THE HIGHLAND CALL

THE HIGHLAND CALL

A Symphonic Play of American History in Two Acts

By PAUL GREEN

WITH HYMN TUNES, FOLKSONGS,
BALLADS, AND DANCE

Chapel Hill
THE UNIVERSITY OF NORTH CAROLINA PRESS
1941

COPYRIGHT, 1941, BY PAUL GREEN

Printed in the United States of America by
VAN REES PRESS · NEW YORK

TO

ANOTHER FLORA,

MY MOTHER

*"While I draw this fleeting breath,
When my eyestrings break in death."*

NOTE

Most of the characters in this play are historical. Sandy and Simey Ochiltree, Dan Murchison, and Peggy MacNeill, however, are entirely imaginary. The two children referred to in the last scene are also imaginary. The legend long existent in North Carolina that a young son and daughter of Flora MacDonald died and were buried at Killiegrey is a legend only and contrary to fact.

For an authoritative account of the life of Flora MacDonald and her immediate relatives, see an article written by Mrs. Dorothy Mackay Quynn in the July, 1941, issue of the *North Carolina Historical Review*.

AUTHOR'S NOTE

Letter to a Friend in Woeful Times

Dear John:

I was glad to get your letter of this week and sorry to hear that you had been under the weather, so to speak. I was sorry also to hear that you had just finished reading *The Lost Colony* and had hurled the book with an oath across the room. All vague and vacuous words, you say, something about an American dream. Well, now I hope with spring in full bloom and the drear-nighted January passed away, these mulligrubs which have infected you will be killed off by the warm light of summer and the "doleful doings" of your mind will give way to the persuasion of flowers and birds and trees and the rich profusion of life pouring out its sweet and everlasting miracle upon the land. That at least should help.

You say, in passing, you are fed up with your environment there—with its clang and clamor, its compressive turmoil of busy and failing lives and wish you were out of it and back among the pines of Carolina. Frankly, John, I hear that sort of story often and remember my father's old saying about cows off yonder having long horns or the grass being greener in another pasture, old sayings that fitted your case the day you left us for your future there, just as they maybe fit you now that you want to come back again. And as for the social ways of a lot of the people around you there, the baiters and the bunders, the manikins and minikins with their psyches and their dogs, the ism-fanatics, the birth-control professionalists, the cultural center aesthetes clasped emptily together for comfort and for art—to list but a few you mention—well, they are to be found everywhere, and you won't escape them by coming here. For as both Brigham Young and Schopenhauer have well shown, along with Solomon, desire is mighty and will prevail, and all kinds of people are forever being dumped into this world. Activity continues, and when sex is off, economics is on, and usually both are putting in full time together.

Yes, like a mighty tree, old life keeps pumping us up in sap from below to spill out as long as time shall last in rich fruitfulness at the top. If some of the twigs do freeze and die, the main and leafy wonder still goes on. And I wouldn't waste too much worry on these perverse and blighted twigs, either. They will rot and fall to the ground to add their pinch of fertilizer to the enrichment of the mystic bush above. This has always been true—as witness the million cold April-bud little poets, artisans, and inventors who have added their small mite to the big things that happen in the world. This is a process known and accepted in the Orient long before the Western World was thought of, and we might do well to consider it. I refer you to the Hindu scriptures which can now be got in a cheap edition of Everyman's Library. You might draw some comfort from them. You know we used to talk a lot about these things when we were students here at the university. I have discovered the book since then.

Now, this all sounds a bit hard-boiled and unsympathetic

AUTHOR'S NOTE

—like a kind of let-things-wag-as-they-will philosophy. I don't mean it that way. I believe that the burning bush or green tree of life—use what figure you will—is endowed with the miracle of consciousness, of emotion, mind and will—and all of us its parts have the power and the bounden duty to help it grow into the world as a thing of beauty forever. That is not only the opportunity and urge of man but his instinctive joy also. There are failings away all along the line, of course, like those you mention above and like those we see every day in any forest. And it has to be so because of an infinity of environmental and hereditary factors which can never wholly be made to behave. But the main body of the tree, of humanity, does not fail and never will; only the bitten twigs and sunless branches die. And when you cry out in your middle-aged distress along with H. G. Wells and others that all is confusion and despair in the world and you would fain rest from it and give over, I know you are wrong and hasten once more for my own clarification and your encouragement to tell you so. I have a sort of abdominal philosophy, an inner witness as it were, that testifies even in the small hours to me that the course of man is upward and not downward. For in the first place man wills it so, and in the second it is the way all things in the large seem fated to proceed. It has taken me a long time to throw off the pessimism our professors of rationalistic philosophy and science taught me as a student, and maybe if you thought around a while you would find some of their old wayward words still whispering to you from the subconscious dark. In these latter days, to repeat, I have found a deeper wisdom than theirs among the Hindus, in certain of the New Testament scriptures such as the first chapter of *John* and the seventh chapter of *Romans,* and in Greek philosophers like Parmenides, Heraclitus, and Plotinus. All of these feel, know and affirm a righteous logic in the universe—a logos, a principle of goodness which nothing can destroy for man except man himself, and he will not do it because he cannot prevail upon himself to so deny himself. In particular and perverted cases, yes, but never in the main body of the tree of humanity. Do not all men of whatever creed or calling as a rule appeal to this goodness—this ethic principle? It is their light, the guide by which they act and do their business. Their ways of finding it are different, and in this difference they often mistake the lesser good for the greater, and as a consequence wars and killings and grievous things continue to happen among us. But these too will pass away—in a long time, a long, long time. Here the challenge is sharpest for our so-called educators and political leaders. Let them get busy and help to shorten that time and so save suffering, but not by graphs and tables and edicts from above. Oh, no! Only by the wisdom of an understanding and loving heart. How then, you say, can new hearts be given to these so diseased ones except by cutting out the old and inserting the new, and then the body dies? Apart from all cuttings, let that body die. Thereafter we shall consider.

And then after deploring the condition of the world and your especial section of it, you say in your letter that you are wretched over the breakdown of American ideals in these latter days. Nay, you go further and declare that these woeful times have proved too clearly that the American system of thought, its democracy, is an idle dream talked about a great deal but never proved, and now with the avalanche of totalitarianism rolling toward us we have nothing with which to meet the enemy, no real defense against him. Here in your letter you wax lyrical with

AUTHOR'S NOTE

pessimism and doubt. America has never done anything high and ideal in the history of the world, you say. We have always been a dog-eat-dog nation if the truth were acknowledged, and before we can get anywhere we've got to recognize ourselves for what we are—a selfish, money-getting, sharp-trading land of usurers. We have no muscle, no stamina. Far better if we had a hard mailed fist at this doleful hour. Ah, and what have the foolish poets sung so long?—you ask—"When in the course of human events—," "Certain inalienable rights"—"Government of the people, by the people, and for the people."

Words, words, you say. Yes, and yet more words.

Out of the rich and deep-bosomed earth,
Mother of all, life-giving and bountiful,
Thou builder and thou leveler,
For thee these words.

Shall not the stones speak, the towering craggy trees
Watchfully waiting on the western hills—
The soft-reeded rivers, the valleys and the springs,
And all of man's making, the roads and the bridges,
Beams and girders and the reaching cables—
The walls and the towers, the fences and the wayfares—
Are these dead and voiceless things empty of meaning?

The scythe drops down, the hammer nerveless drops,
The plow and the shovel wait unused and still,
The weeds take them, the roots thread their sightless
    sockets through,

The handles shaped to human hands dissolve in dust,
And the fierce and clamorous strength that used them once,
That ditched and dug and built with them there,
Is gone forever in the tomb.
What then shall their dreaming and their purpose all be lost,
The head of agony upon the pillow turned for naught?

AUTHOR'S NOTE

Out of the tomb is there no voice now,
There by the low enclosing wall of quiet,
Silent in the evening's grievous hush?
All is muted in the fresh upflaming morn,
All tongueless waits the lordly mountain top.
Shall these souls be bound in the tremulous chains of the
    starlight,
Or dust and ashes befoul the bright head of beauty?
O fading footsteps lost forever,
O eloquent lips and passionate hearts,
And gesturing final hands!—
Shall these forever be as if they'd never been?

Nay, cry out the roll-call of their prideful names,
Wake with the reveille of our buoyant song
These that lie forgotten and foregone.
Now all our walking is the paths they trod,
Our speech their same shaped mouth and tuneful tongue,
Our gestures still the same strong-fingered hand,
Plucking the bouquets, firing the guns,
Building and shaping and creating in their stead.
So thus the dead do live in us again,
And we the living honorably may die.

I believe that, John, and I'm sure you are wrong—not because you attack Jefferson, Lincoln, and any multitude of others, but because you attack the deep and human vision by which we live. America has done great things and will do other great things, noble things. It's not all words. And what great things beyond the dollar and the dime? you ask with weary and doubting irony.

All right, then, the conquering of this vast wilderness of the Western World. It was not any easy thing to do, but our forefathers did it—slowly step by step, ax blow by ax blow and furrow by furrow. At first only the precarious

AUTHOR'S NOTE

hold upon the eastern fringes of this land was theirs. Then with incredible hardship and toil from father to son and to other sons they made their way inland, up into the hills, to the mountains, over the mountains, across the rivers and the plains to still other mountains north and south till another ocean three thousands miles away was reached. You know all these facts from your history books. And out of this wide and boundless struggle with nature, a strong self-reliance was developed, untrammeled by any clan intrigues, fealties and Old World loyalties of Europe. The mother country was far away, and day by day grew farther both in space and memory, and these her children, as is the course of things, came to be men in their own right and jealous of their hard-won prerogatives, feeling a proud ownership in the place and product of their toils. And as they depended on their skill, their industry and strength without appeal or favor from others, so did they grow to resent exploitation by any outside authority. It's true as you in your present state of discouragement are quick to point out, these pioneers in conquering the wilderness did, from the very abundance of the land and its resources, set the habit of waste and carelessness which has come so evilly down to this day. We must remedy such mistakes and are doing it. Even here there is work to do instead of repining like the insect in the fable.

Then there followed the creation of the democratic ideal of government. Try as you will you can't laugh or sneer that off. For centuries men had dreamed of such an ideal, had written and preached about it—Confucius, Plato, Jesus, John Locke, and countless others—but none had ever found the proper statement for it nor the time and place to put it into practice. And when on that long-ago day of June 12th, 1776, the Virginia House of Burgesses adopted the Bill of Rights as finally drawn up by the leading thinkers of that colony, something new had begun among men. I believe that. With this basic statement made, the Declaration of Independence and the Constitution of the United States soon were derived. Here at last and for the first time in the history of the world was begun a system of government based upon the recognition of the absolute worth of the individual, one declaring that each and every man is an ultimate reality in himself and as such has certain inalienable rights that go with being a man. Nothing shall take these rights away from him. And to protect him in these rights, and for this reason only, governments can be said to rightfully exist. He shall be secure in his person and the earnings of his hands and brain. No one shall unjustly imprison him or visit excessive punishment upon him. He shall be free to go and come as he pleases, to speak his mind openly and freely, to think as he pleases, and to worship his God as he sees fit. These are self-evident principles, our forefathers said, and irrespective of color, creed, or previous condition of servitude men everywhere instinctively know them as true. For after all, men are individuals before everything else. Is not their birth, their love, and their death their very own and nobody else's? Can they feel with another's hands, eat with another's mouth, or think with another's mind? No, their very being is their own and theirs alone. Man is who he is and nobody else. Can a child grow into manhood lying in the arms of his father? Or a daughter be more than that on the bosom of her mother? No, they must grow up. In homely phrase, every tub must stand on its own bottom. Democracy is a philosophy fitted to men full grown, men who acknowledge themselves as morally responsible beings as well as free, and who accept the rights

AUTHOR'S NOTE

that go with that responsibility. They accept freedom in terms of responsibility and responsibility in terms of freedom.

And now the abuses. Yes, there are plenty of them. Our vision still exceeds our accomplishment; our reach, our grasp. But thank God we've had the vision, we've had the reach, and day by day we are making progress towards answering the challenge of those living words. And we are doing it from these basic principles beneath, not blindly from above as is the case with too many governments known for the present as totalitarian. Let us try to remember that.

And our pioneer leadership in the creation of this the machine age! Think of that. For the first time in the history of man this country has produced the ultimately perfect servant—call him the cotton gin, the gas engine, electric motor, telephone, talking machine, radio, or what you will. And we have conceived of and created these machines for the service of the individual, the democratic man, as a means of lightening his toil, freeing him from economic slavery for exercise of things of beauty and the spirit and not for uses of hate and death and destruction. We so conceive of them and will as long as our democratic philosophy remains deeply integrated into the bone and blood-beat of our life as it is now. Here again the vision is being abused. Too many of our leaders continue to be sucked in by the pull to exploitation and the main chance. But we must not despair. It takes time, a long, long time for the best to be—a long, long time for the hypocrites, windbags and blackguards to die. But ultimately they will and will receive their fitting reward. No system works perfectly, whatever the first reaches of its dream may proclaim, and the challenge always is towards a more and more perfect fulfillment. To return to my former figure—this growing of the mystic tree into the nobility of full form is a long process. It cannot suddenly be flowered into the sky by any artificial propagation or stimulus. It has to grow from the deep roots below, and this a power-sprung Europe will learn when its crisis is past. It is easy to fight wars, it is hard to dramatize peace. Democracy's business is with the latter even when the militancy of marching feet is required.

No, John, I do not share your discouragement about our country. I am more keenly alive to its greatness now than ever before. All of this turmoil and trouble you speak of had to come. It is the convulsion of a new order coming into the world. And that new order, when the convulsion is finished, will be one nearer democracy than otherwise. Don't scoff, for I am in earnest. It may be called by some other name, but when it comes the individual must have his rightful place in it, must be recognized for what he is as a free soul with certain inalienable rights and responsibilities, or else the convulsion will break out again. Humanity is on the march to freedom, not to slavery, and nothing will stop it. The winning of the wilderness here, the riving out of our constitution, the creation of the machine age are steps towards that world freedom, and as we have been pioneers in the past so must we continue to be in the future. And not until the new international order, in which both individuals and nations have their rightful place, has come to pass can we count the victory ours. And we must strive to spare the blood, John, spare the blood and the tears in that mighty undertaking.

And in that new day this country will begin the fourth great adventure of its history—the adventure of culture. Art, literature, music, philosophy, and true science will

AUTHOR'S NOTE

flourish then as never before. We are ready for them, and you be ready, too, John. Let us both add our sap to the main and leafy wonder, calling out with Whitman—

Give me, O God, to sing that thought,
Give me, give him or her I love this quenchless faith,
In thy ensemble, whatever else withheld withhold not from us
Belief in plan of thee enclosed in time and space,
Health, peace, salvation universal.

And herewith, John, I send you another play of American history, a sort of call to the highlands ahead. You may throw it across the room in disgust like the other one, but in doing so you can only criticize me and not the rightness of the thing I am trying to tell about. Nor will you in any whit diminish the joy I have had in constructing the story and bringing back to life these characters of the long ago—with something of their faith, their vision and their cheerful song. Bear with me and read it through if you can.

So farewell, and send me a copy of your new book when it comes out. And don't forget the Hindu scriptures.

Ever,

P. G.

CONTENTS

AUTHOR'S NOTE	ix
THE HIGHLAND CALL	1
THE HIGHLAND CALL SONGBOOK	197
LIST OF SONGS	199
WORDS AND MUSIC	205
GLOSSARY	273
PROGRAM	
The Fayetteville Historical Celebration, 1939	275

THE HIGHLAND CALL

THE CHARACTERS

Mr. Mac, *an antiquarian in the valley, the narrator*
Flora MacDonald, *a Scotch heroine and British loyalist*
Allan MacDonald, *her husband*
Alexander MacDonald, *Flora's son*
James MacDonald, *a younger son*
Anne MacLeod, *Flora's daughter*
Alexander MacLeod, *Anne's husband*
Peggy MacNeill, *Flora's niece*
Donald MacDonald, *Peggy's fiancé*
Dan Murchison, *a shepherd lad, later indentured to Allan MacDonald*
Sandy Ochiltree, *one of the MacDonald servants*
Simey Ochiltree, *Sandy's twin brother*
Jennie Bhan MacNeill, *a Scotch matriarch of the Cape Fear Valley*
Colonel Alexander MacAllister, *a Whig leader*
Farquhar Campbell, *a political leader in Cross Creek*
Hugh MacDonald, *Flora's stepfather*
Colonel Cotton, *a Tory leader*
Reverend John MacLeod, *a Presbyterian minister at old Barbecue Church*

A chorus of singers, a British officer, a Highland shepherd, a ship's captain, the mayor of Campbelltown, Whig and Tory neighbors—soldiers, men, women, and children.

THE TIME

The latter part of the eighteenth century.

THE PLACE

Scotland and America.

ACT ONE

SCENE 1

When the audience is assembled in the theater, the organist in the loge at the left begins playing the overture. He plays first a skirl of bagpipe notes, then passes into the old hymn tune of "St. Anne's." When that is concluded he crashes into a heavy dead march from "The Highland Widow's Lament" and ends finally in a wide-spaced chord introduction to the Flora MacDonald song. During the overture the lights go down to half-dim, and as the organist builds towards his finale, they sink into the darkness. In the meantime the chorus has filed into the pit. The organ holds its loud final chord and then accompanies the chorus as it stands and sings.

Chorus

Far over yon hills o' the heather sae green,
And down by the corrie that sings by the sea,
The bonnie young Flora sat sighing her lane,
The dew on her plaid and the tear in her e'e.
She looked at the boat wi' the breezes that swung,
Away on the waves like a bird on the main;
And aye, as it lessen'd she sigh'd as she sung,
"Fareweel to the lad I shall ne'er see again!
Fareweel to my hero, the gallant and young,
Fareweel to the lad I shall ne'er see again!"

At the end of the song the light dies from the chorus and comes on in the loge at the right. The figure of a man is seen standing there. This is Mr. Mac, and he is a kindly common-sense person enough, though his garb seems to be a little queer, and his make-up somewhat out of the ordinary. He is dressed in a clerical collar and tie and a coat of plaided stuff, in the buttonhole of which a spray of heather is stuck. He is bareheaded and his face, though ascetic in its thinness, is brown as a berry and marked with signs of exposure to rain and wind and sun. His thin hair is neatly brushed over and across the bare ridge of his fine head, and a scraggly gray moustache adds to the fatherliness of his manner. He looks out over the audience, smiles slightly, and gives a little nod as the organ stops. Then he lays his hand on the pulpit or lectern erected in the loge for his convenience, and speaks.

Mr. Mac
(*In a quiet, even voice.*)
Good evening, everybody. I'm glad to see so many of our good Scotch people and their friends here tonight.
(*Looking out into the audience.*)
Good evening, Janet, and you, too, Hector. And how are you, Mr. MacKinnon? A hearty welcome to you all. And we hope you are going to enjoy the play. I say "we"—because the author has written a part in it for me. I am the narrator or commentator, and I'm going to give you something of the history of events and background of the story as we go along. The people call me Mr. Mac, and the author said he chose me to act this Scotch part because he found out that I was not only one of the god-blessed Macs but also something of a historian. I know I am blessed, my name is Mac, and perhaps I am a sort of historian, for I have tramped or ridden up and down the

THE HIGHLAND CALL

whole width and breadth of the Cape Fear River Valley, from Smith's Island at the mouth to the old town of Haywood at the head two hundred miles away. Of recent years, too, I have been a preacher, and at one time or another have held services in nearly every church from Barbecue to Brunswick. There's hardly a square mile of the some eight thousand that make up this valley that I haven't visited—and looked for old tombstones and the weed-covered foundations of some ancient house. And in my wanderings I have gathered many an item of local and general interest, many an old land deed, or book or letter, legend and story, and many a fine ballad and song and proverb.

I know this section of the country, and as I know it, so do I love it beyond all places of the earth. For there are no finer people anywhere, none with a richer past, none I hope with a greater future, and certainly none with a dwelling place more beautiful—a land of flowers and trees and water and singing birds, of flaming sunsets, mellow fields and autumn skies.

And our people came into this valley more than a hundred and fifty years ago—aye, some of them more than two hundred years ago, and settled, built their homes in the wilderness here, laid out roads and towns, cleared the forest and raised their schools and churches to the knowledge and worship of God. And as they lived, struggled, and died for the cause they believed in, so let it be our privilege to hold in remembrance the heritage of that struggle which they have left to us. And that's why we are gathered here tonight—to remember. In humility and prayer let us—

    (*He bows his head a moment, the light dims somewhat, and the organ plays the old hymn of "Dundee" while the chorus sings from the darkness.*)

Chorus

O God, our help in ages past,
Our hope for years to come,
Our shelter from the stormy blast,
And our eternal home.

Time, like an ever-rolling stream,
Bears all its sons away;
They fly, forgotten, as a dream
Dies at the opening day.

Before the hills in order stood,
Or earth received her frame,
From everlasting Thou art God,
To endless years the same.

(When the hymn is finished, Mr. Mac raises his head, and the light brightens again.)

Mr. Mac

And now to begin our play. Let us go back into the reaches of the past, into Scotland at the middle of the eighteenth century. Here the people for generations had waged a struggle against England for the control of power. But mutual strife, wars among the clans, and divided interests had weakened them, and the last pretender to the Scottish throne, Prince Charles Edward of the House of Stuart, was finally and disastrously defeated at the battle of Culloden in 1745. Among those who aided in this tragic struggle was the great MacDonald clan, Lords of the Western Isles. And none was more active in the cause than the Scotch heroine, Flora MacDonald. For like many another

THE HIGHLAND CALL

she saw in Prince Charles not only the king of Scotland but the rightful ruler of Britain itself. And through him the true glory of the empire was to continue across the world. But the power of arms decided otherwise, and her last gesture in defeat was to save the prince from capture by the British and help him escape to France. For this she was tried and imprisoned in the Tower of London but later pardoned. And now with the new order of empire established and the sorrowful story of blood and war foregone, she along with her countrymen took up the duty of devoted allegiance in the cause of a united Britain, and in an oath of blood they swore—

(*He gestures towards the center curtain, bows his head again and retires. The light has been coming slowly up on the stage, spotting in dim outlines a table at which an English officer is sitting. A clerk is beside him with a great open book, and behind the officer two red-coated soldiers are faintly outlined with bayonetted muskets. In front of the officer a poor Highland farmer is standing, his hat tucked under his arm. A little boy about seven or eight years old is with him and holding to his hand.*)

Officer

(*Concluding.*)
I swear.

Man

(*Repeating.*)
I swear.
(*Pulling his dirk from his belt he makes a pricking motion at his wrist.*)

Boy

(*With a cry.*)
Father—

Man

A mark with my own blood—aye—

Boy

(*Vehemently, at the officer, his face quivering.*)
You're hurting my father.

Officer

Keep him quiet.
(*A soldier steps forward into the light and stands by the boy.*)

Man

Ne'er mind, Dan.
(*He puts his finger to his wrist and marks in the great book. The little boy bows his head, his shoulders shaking with repressed sobs.*)

Officer

Like this mark, John Murchison, your sacred oath will never be erased—

Man

(*Bitterly.*)
Sacred all right—for with my family murdered, my house burnt, and my few poor acres ruined I have no heart to break it now.

Officer
So does it happen to all enemies of His Majesty—

Man
Yea, and out of all this someday I'll go—go where my boy can grow up and have a chance. We will, Danny boy. There in America beyond the sea—

Officer
Your knife.

Man
Sir, I am a shepherd—it is the last tool left to me—

Officer
There!—
  (*The man lays it down on the table.*)

Man
  (*Taking the boy by the hand.*)
Come on, son.
  (*But the boy springs forward and grabs up the knife. The soldier seizes him and after a short struggle gets it from him.*)

Officer
  (*Angrily.*)
Even the children suck hatred here with their milk. Take him out.

Boy
Give it back to him—give it—

MAN
(*Putting his arm around him and leading him off.*)
Nothing to do about it, Dan, nothing. Come on, we got to go back to work—
(*They disappear into the shadow at the left.*)

OFFICER
(*Curtly.*)
Next.

CLERK
MacDonald.
(*Allan and Flora MacDonald come out of the gloom at the right and approach the table. Allan is a tall grave Scotchman in his early thirties and is dressed in ordinary but good English clothes of the period. Flora MacDonald is of about the same age, though looking much younger. She is slender and somewhat below medium height, with a mobile spirited face and wide dark eyes. She wears a shawl over her head.*)

OFFICER
(*Rising and bowing.*)
At last.

FLORA
You were expecting us?

OFFICER
Hoping and expecting, madam.

ALLAN
We will take the oath.

WOOTTEN-MOULTON

FLORA MacDONALD (*played by Katherine Moran*)

FLORA MACDONALD (*played by Katherine Moran*) and ALLAN MACDONALD (*played by Pendleton Harrrison*) take the oath of allegiance to Britain's king

The girls of Campbelltown, Scotland, greet the mayor (*played by Allan Frank*)

Officer

Aye and a great day it is.
 (*Bowing again slightly as Allan bows.*)
And now the last stronghold of rebellion will be broken in these Western Isles.

Flora

And 'tis right. Our cause is ended now.

Officer

And in his majesty's name I commend you for this act. England is proud of you.

Flora

This oath is not for England alone, sir, but for the empire —an empire in which my native Scotland shall have her rightful place.

Officer

You are correct, madam.
 (*As if quoting.*)
United we stand—divided we fall—our new watchword of brotherhood.

Flora

Aye.

Allan

Aye.

Officer

This for you.
 (*He hands Flora an opened letter.*)

FLORA
(*Without taking it.*)
It has been read.

OFFICER
True—

FLORA
I recognize the seal. You can destroy it.

ALLAN
(*Quickly.*)
Read it, Flora, it is from him.

FLORA
(*Bowing her head a bit.*)
Yes, from the Prince. I shall not read it.

OFFICER
He calls upon all his loyal followers and you to refuse the oath. His day is not set. He will yet rise again.
(*Mockingly.*)
From his drunken hiding place in France he will rise again.

FLORA
(*Sadly.*)
He will never rise again.
(*Reaching over she takes the letter and tears it in two, dropping the pieces on the floor.*)
We must follow a greater and a better cause. I know it now. The oath, please.

THE HIGHLAND CALL

Officer

Bravo. Your hands.
(Allan and Flora raise their hands.—Quoting.)
I, Allan MacDonald of Kingsboro and I, Flora MacDonald of Skye—
(They repeat the words in union.)
—do swear and as I shall answer to my God in the great day of judgment—
(As they repeat this, Sandy Ochiltree, dressed in the well-worn tartan of the MacDonald clan, edges forward in the light and watches them breathlessly. He is a thin middle-aged fellow and wears an old tam-o'-shanter with two crow's feathers stuck in it. Hugged up against him he carries an old bagpipe strung with a strap around his shoulders. Coming timidly and fearfully behind him is his twin brother Simey, a sturdy, bareheaded peasant fellow dressed in a moth-eaten jacket, rough trousers and heavy shoes.)
—solemnly take oath that I shall never bear arms against the rightful king of Britain—
(They repeat this.)
—that I shall forego all action, all tokens and symbols of separation—
(They repeat.)
—and may I never see my wife (husband) and children, father, mother, loved ones or relations—
(They repeat.)
—may I be killed in battle as a coward and lie without Christian sacrament—
(They repeat and Sandy shudders.)
—unburied and forgot far from the graves of my forefathers and kindred—
(They repeat.)

—may all this come across me if I break my oath—in the name of my king and Almighty God, Amen.
(*They repeat this and Allan pulls out his knife.*)

Sandy

(*Piteously.*)
Not that, master. Spare the blood.
(*Springing forward in front of Allan.*)
By Saint Jeremy's beard, you shan't harm my master.

Officer

(*Now noticing him for the first time.*)
Who is this bold fellow?

Sandy

Me, Sandy Ochiltree.
(*Edging away from the officer's threatening looks.*)
Oh, please, your honor, don't make him stick himself.

Officer

Arrest him!
(*The soldier steps over and claps his hand on Sandy's shoulder.*)
What means this traitorous clothing?

Sandy

I ain't got nothing else to wear, your reverence.

Officer

(*To the soldiers.*)
Strip him and find him some breeks.

SANDY
That's indecent, sir—for me it is. Dadlem it, I ain't never wore no britches in all my life. Oh, master Allan.
(*To Flora.*)
Save me, ma'am.
(*Simey begins to fill the air with belligerent gesticulations.*)

ALLAN
He is one of my servants—

SANDY
And sworn to protect 'em till death, I am, sir. But as for protecting myself—a coward, sir—coward down to the ground and weak as stump water.

ALLAN
And this is his afflicted brother.

SANDY
Aye, poor fellow, afflicted in his head, and from the day of birth dumb as the rocks of Dunvegan. He's my twin, sir, and all his words were give to me.

OFFICER
And where went the looks of both ye?

SANDY
Uhm—
(*Simey comes up to him and puts his arm protectingly around him.*)
Ne'er ye mind, Simey boy, they'd not hurt poor old Sandy.

Officer

Yea, we would!
    (*Sandy jumps.*)
There's a royal edict reissued against the clan dress—good English dress is ordered.

Allan

He shall be outfitted properly—as soon as possible.

Sandy

Oh—I'll ketch my death in them things, master. They'll gall and skin me till I'm destroyed—

Officer

Take the knife and mark this book with your traitorous blood—
    (*With a squeak, Sandy starts towards the right but one of the soldiers heads him off.*)

Allan

I'll vouch for him.
    (*The officer stares at Sandy a moment as he shivers and shakes.*)

Officer

Are you a musician?

Sandy

    (*Eagerly.*)
And one of the best pipers in the county and my valor proved on Culloden Field. A piper is a sacred soul, sir. It's bad luck to harm a piper.

Officer

Sacred or profane, do you swear to serve your king?

Sandy

Yessir, yessir, I'll take all the oaths under heaven's high arch—but please sir, don't make me damage myself with a knife.

Officer

Hold up your hand.
    (*He does so.*)
Higher!
    (*He reaches up on tiptoe.*)
Drop it!
    (*He does.*)
Now you are sworn, and if ever you break this oath I'll send all the witches of the Western Isles to dig your eyes out, to cut you in small pieces, and boil you in burning pitch.

Sandy

Lord, have mercy—

Officer

Begone—
    (*Sandy flies away into the darkness at the left followed by Simey. The officer turns to Allan and Flora.*)
You are lucky in him—he's a humorous fool.
    (*Nodding.*)
The book—
    (*Allan makes the pricking motion at his wrist, and dipping a pen against the wound signs the open page.*)
And you, madam, are excepted in this.

Flora

I am not—
> (*She takes Allan's knife.*)

Allan

Flora—

Flora

> (*Pricking herself and signing her name.*)

Let it not be said that I failed in any whit the cause which now I follow—this the seventeenth day of October, 1752.

Officer

> (*Admiringly.*)

I am proud to be a countryman to you. And now in his majesty's name I commend you. May the blessings of peace come to you and yours and you be restored in all that you have lost. Farewell. Farewell to you, sir.

Allan and Flora

Farewell.
> (*They go away into the darkness at the left, the two soldiers holding their muskets in salute. The officer stares after her.*)

Officer

A brave and noble woman.
> (*The soldiers lower their guns again.*)

Clerk

Aye.
> (*Laconically.*)

And has great hopes—something about a vast empire.

THE HIGHLAND CALL

Officer

(*Barking out.*)

Next.

(*The light fades away from the scene and rises on the chorus as the organ strikes up in "Wae's Me for Prince Charlie." The chorus stands and sings with heavy mournfulness, accompanied by the organ.*)

Chorus

A wee bird came to our ha' door,
He warbled sweet and clearly.
And aye the o'ercome o' his sang
Was "Wae's me for Prince Charlie!"
Oh when I heard the bonnie, bonnie bird,
The tears cam drapping rarely.
I took my bonnet off my head,
For well I loved Prince Charlie.

"Dark night cam on, the tempest roar'd,
Loud o'er the hills an' valleys,
An' where was't that your Prince lay down,
Wha's hame should been a palace?
He row'd him in a Highland plaid,
That cover'd him but sparely,
And slept beneath a bush o' broom—
Oh wae's me for Prince Charlie!"

(*The light dies from the chorus and comes up on Mr. Mac again as he stands in the loge at the right.*)

Mr. Mac

And so with the taking of the oath, the strife and hate between England and Scotland ended, and a new day of union and brotherhood began. But the sweet rewards of peace were long in coming—longer than anyone dreamed of on that particular day in 1752 when Allan and Flora MacDonald signed the book. The ravages of fire and sword had seared the heart of Scotland, and in that land of brief summer and lengthy winter the recovery of the earth is slow. Too, the new kingdom was beset by outside enemies on the continent and by constant upheavals of political and economic factions within. And famine and drought and the pestilence of nature kept their everlasting and accustomed toll.

And the days passed, the months passed, the years went and came, and the people suffered under their bitter poverty. And many died from the hardships of their lot—one of them being John Murchison, who found no new life beyond the sea but rather the darkness of a Highland grave, leaving his orphan son, Dan Murchison, to grow up a shepherd lad on the stony hills of Skye.

And hundreds, yes, thousands of people migrated to North Carolina, some to escape the fearful oath of allegiance, some to escape starvation, and still others to aid in their dream of an ever-growing British empire. And they all sent back glowing accounts of this new Cape Fear Valley, with its balmy climate, fertile soil, great forests, and grassy uplands and reedy bottoms where their cattle grew fat in winter and summer. During the years 1746-1774 some fifteen thousand left their native land and settled in this section, and on an afternoon in August, 1774, Flora and her family arrived at the little seaport of Campbelltown in southern Scotland where a ship waited to take them to the new world.

(*While Mr. Mac is speaking the light comes partly up on the center stage.*)

SCENE 2

The wharf at Campbelltown, in Scotland. At the left front and running diagonally back into the shadows at the right rear is a stout wattle or paling fence about the height of a man's shoulders, and with sharp-pointed tips. A gate at the left front opens through it. At the right front is an old barrel or cask, and a few other casks and boxes are at the back. Old Sandy Ochiltree is sitting on a bundle of baggage in front of the gate. He is much the same as when we saw him last, except older, being now about sixty and with a few wrinkles in his face. He wears an old pair of voluminous breeches over his kilt, and his tam with its two crow's feathers still adorns his weathered head. His old bagpipe is slung across his shoulder. He is holding a needle and thread in one hand and a ragged shoe in his other. On a bundle of baggage at the right front sits his twin brother Simey. His gray hair is a little longer and more ragged, and his clothes somewhat the worse for wear than before. A homemade Indian bow is strung over his shoulder, and he holds a pet bantam rooster in the crook of his arm. A low wailing or keen of women's voices in "The Highland Widow's Lament" is heard in the distance at the left rear and continues off and on through the scene. The organ has begun softly playing the introduction to Sandy's song. The light is full up on the stage now. The organ grows somewhat more insistent.

SANDY
(Breaking into croaking song and sewing while he sings.)

In Scotland there lived a gay young widow,
And glittering gold had she, had she,
And she was well-courted by all the laddies,
Including a coof of a fool, that's me.

Her hair it was black, her eyes were sparkling,
Her lips they were ripe and red, so red,
And weary the hours I watched at her window,
With an aching heart and woeful head.

Ochon and alas—

(*His song dies into a doleful whistle. The sound of the keening comes in from the distance. The organ fades out and Sandy sews away. He turns and calls in irritation towards the keening.*)

Whist ye old grisly hags! Ye'll rouse everybody on the ship with your bedlam racket and screeching.
 (*Wagging his head in mockery.*)
Oh, and it's me poor bonnie boys and wee pritty lasses set to sail across the wide ocean. Ochon—ochrie! Our hearths be empty and desolate, and the cold ashes have smothered the flame of our joy—And why shouldn't they be sailing away? There's nothing here in this woeful land of Scotland but rocks and wind and a power of raging waters between the hills. And the people like sheep coughing out their lives in the freezing fogs. Whist, I tell ye.
 (*Biting off the thread, he bends down and begins putting on his shoe. The keening dies away on the wind somewhat. Two redcoat British soldiers come in, carrying their bayonetted muskets. They stop beside Sandy.*)

First Soldier

Heigh, old fellow.

Sandy

(*Springing up.*)
What is it? Oh—the soldiers.

First Soldier

Yes, the soldiers. And what are you doing here?

Sandy

Minding my own business.

Second Soldier

And who is he?

Sandy

My brother Simey—harmless as a dove and all set to sail away to the Indian land—see his bow?
(*He sits down again.*)

First Soldier

Uhm, poor Indians. Have you seen a stray young fellow come by here?

Sandy

I have not.

Second Soldier

(*Somewhat easy-going.*)
We're looking for one Dan Murchison. Do you know him?

SANDY

(*Narrowly.*)
You mean an old fellow with one eye and a monstrous great beard on him. Aye, poor Dan.

FIRST SOLDIER

We do not, we mean young Dan Murchison, a wild farmer lad. He's wanted for the king's army.

SANDY

Lordy-mercy!

FIRST SOLDIER

He's hid on that ship.

SANDY

He is not—He's back home tending his sheep this minute on the Isle of Skye and lonesome for me and Simey right now.

SECOND SOLDIER

But he's been traced here.

SANDY

(*Shaking his head vehemently.*)
Nunh-unh. All these years he's wanted to go to America—and how could he—him like the barefooted king of Norway, naked as a yard dog?

SECOND SOLDIER

(*Indulgently.*)
And who was the barefoot king of Norway, old man?

Sandy

One Magnus, he was, and all writ down. A song was made of it. I can sing it.
   (*Beginning.*)
"Old Magnus he lived high up in the mountains"—

First Soldier

No, not now.
   (*To the second.*)
Watch here.
   (*He starts towards the gate, but Sandy springs in front of him.*)

Sandy

You canna go in there.

First Soldier

And why not?

Sandy

Because the captain told me to guard this gate. He's gone with my mistress to say farewell to the old castle—
   (*Gesturing towards the rear.*)
—they'll be here any minute.

First Soldier

Is your mistress by chance Flora MacDonald?

Sandy

Aye, the same that saved bonnie Prince Charlie and made you English a laughing stock forever.

First Soldier

Yeh, a laughing stock!

(Reaching out he flings Sandy from the gate and strides on through.)

Sandy

(Calling furiously after him.)

You'll ketch it. A captain's ship is sacred and it's bad luck to touch it.

(He sits disgustedly down on the baggage and fans himself with his old tam.)

Second Soldier

(After a moment.)

So you're sailing off to America?

Sandy

I am—like everybody else, me and Simey.

Second Soldier

And who sails with you?

Sandy

Master and mistress and the family. And Mistress Peggy MacNeill too—to be married in time beyond the sea to Master Donald that waits for her.

Second Soldier

(Teasingly.)

I hear tell there's buffalo critters in that strange country big as a house and bears that swallow a man at a gulp.

MR. MAC (*played by Earl Wynn*)

Dan Murchison (*played by John Straub*) begs for passage to America

SANDY

No.

SECOND SOLDIER

And Indians that slip up on you in the dead of night, and take your hair, dripping wet with blood and half your head with it.

SANDY

No, I tell ye.

SECOND SOLDIER

That's what I've heard.

SANDY

Then ye've heard wrong, for North Caroliny is a land of sunshine and hanging fruits and tobacco and good snuff. Don't all the MacNeills and the MacAllisters say so? And they've been there for years. And we're going over and jine 'em and help build the empire. Bless the Lord.

SECOND SOLDIER

Amen.
    (*Slyly.*)
You're a sworn man, ain't you?

SANDY

I am that. I took an oath after the Battle of Culloden. Long as my arm it was, bloody and frightful.

SECOND SOLDIER

Then you'll be damned for lying about this Dan Murchison.

SANDY

I ain't lying, I tell you. He's at home, mourning by the grave of his father. Poor boy.

(The first soldier comes striding in from the left.)

I saw a fellow turn behind that fish house down there. Come on.

(They hurry off at the right. Sandy stands up and stares after them.)

SANDY

(Calling through his cupped hands in a whisper.)

Run, Dan, run!—

(Shaking his head, he turns back to his seat.)

That's him, Simey, and they'll ketch him. Ahm, he's followed us here. It's Mistress Peggy MacNeill he's a-follering. Fool.

SIMEY

(Grunting and pointing off at the left.)

Unh—unh—

SANDY

Whist, I tell you—we'll be on them frightful waters soon enough.

(The organ suddenly begins playing a swirl of music, and the bright gay voices of young girls are heard off at the right. Several girls enter dancing and skipping around another girl in their midst.)

GIRLS

(Now going around in a circle, singing.)

Go choose your east, go choose your west, he's the one that you love best.

(Clapping their hands and calling out with light fluttering cries.)

Peggy—Peggy—Good-bye, Peggy—Bless you and happy may you be!

Peggy
(*A beautiful and spirited girl, flushed in her happy embarrassment.*)
Thank you—thank you! And I'll be sending you presents from Carolina—
(*Sandy opens the gate and bows with a wide smile. Then they are all suddenly silent as the mayor of Campbelltown—a huge-stomached, kindly man comes in, carrying a package before him. With him is a minister and several townsmen and townswomen.*)

Mayor
(*Stopping and smiling benignantly around him.*)
It warms me in my heart to see ye all so happy in this hour of farewell.

Voice
Hooray for the mayor!

Crowd
(*Cheering.*)
'Ray for the mayor—'ray, 'ray!
(*The mayor bows about him in recognition of their applause.*)

Mayor
(*Lifting his hand.*)
Friends, many a time I have been on this wharf saying farewell to my neighbors and my friends who have gone forth across the ocean to America. But never has it been

my privilege to say farewell to a happier and more illustrious company than is gathering here today.
> (*A stalwart young fellow with a mop of hair over his forehead and an old cap pulled down over his eyes comes in at the right carrying a string of fish.*)

Young Man
(*In a high, singing voice.*)
Fi—s—sh for sale! Who wants any fish? On—ly—tuppence the six of them—Fresh fish! And ee-ee-eels a special—tee-ee! Fresh—

Mayor
(*Angrily.*)
Take your wares off at once—
> (*The young man comes on across the scene. Old Sandy opens the gate and stands by it.*)

Sandy
You heard his honor.
> (*He begins gesturing excitedly with his thumb towards the gate at the left. Peggy MacNeill is standing close to him now and she recognizes the young man.*)

Peggy
Dan!

Dan
(*Calling again.*)
Ee—ee—eels a specialtee!

SANDY

The poor folks on shipboard are hungry for fish, young man.

(*He hurries Dan towards the gate. The second soldier appears beyond and stands waiting. Dan turns and wanders back across the scene towards the right calling his wares.*)

DAN

Fish—fresh fish—
(*The first soldier appears in front of him with his musket. He looks sharply at Dan and stops him.*)

FIRST SOLDIER

What's your name?

DAN

(*Holding up the string of fish.*)
Only tuppence the six of them—
(*He sticks them close to the soldier's nose.*)

MAYOR

Off with ye!
(*Dan goes on out calling his wares in the distance.*)

FIRST SOLDIER

(*To Sandy.*)
He looks like our man. Does anyone here know him?
(*There is no answer. The soldiers hurry on out.*)

PEGGY

Stop the soldiers, your honor. That lad has done no wrong.

MAYOR

Who is he?

PEGGY

He is a poor shepherd lad from our Isle of Skye.

MAYOR

(*Shaking his head.*)
They are the king's men.

PEGGY

But—they have no cause to arrest him.

MAYOR

Then he can be freed.
(*The organ gives a flourish of trumpets and the mayor looks off to the right, as do the others, and bows low.*)

PEOPLE

(*Cheering and waving their bonnets and handkerchiefs.*)
MacDonald! MacDonald! 'Ray! 'Ray!
(*The MacDonald cortege enters at the right. In the front marches a young man bearing a British flag, and behind him Flora MacDonald and her husband Allan. They have both aged somewhat but carry themselves with energy and decision. Allan's hair has grayed and his face is marked with lines, but Flora's face is still youthful in its matronly firmness, and her figure trim and neat, though her eyes are more often*

THE HIGHLAND CALL

troubled with a brooding thoughtfulness now. Behind them come the rest of the family—the daughter, Anne, with her tall middle-aged husband, Alexander MacLeod; old Kate MacDonald, the nurse, carrying a baby in her arms; and the two sons, Alexander and James MacDonald. They are all wearing good but sober English clothes of the times. As they approach, Sandy springs up and shouts out the slogan of the MacDonald Clanranalds.)

Sandy

Dh'aindheoin co theiraidhe!
(Several of the people repeat the cry, and the organ strikes up "Hail to the Chief." The chorus sings, and the crowd joins its vocables in the melody.)

Chorus

Hail to the chief who in triumph advances,
Honored and blest be the evergreen pine.
Long may the tree in his banner that glances
Flourish the shelter and grace of our line.
    Heav'n send it happy dew,
    Earth send it sap anew,
Gladly to burgeon and broadly to grow;
    While every Highland glen
    Sends our shout back again—
Roderick Alpine dhu ho! ieroe!

(Flora, her husband, and the others receive their songs with nods and smiles as the mayor steps out in front of them.)

Mayor

(Holding up his hand again at the end of the song and addressing Flora and Allan.)

My lady, and you, sir,—this humble village and the county of Kintyre, aye all Scotland herself, join me at this hour in saying hail and farewell.

Allan

(In slow words.)

We thank you and the people, one and all.

(Flora murmurs her thanks and stands looking before her.)

Mayor

And let me say that the story of your heroism and bravery in the service of your country will live as long as honor lives.

(Allan looks fondly at his wife.)

—And in the name of our ancient heritage, in the name of yonder ruined castle that looks down upon us—we say Godspeed and bless you. And now as a token of our admiration and esteem, we the people of Campbelltown with our small means do offer this little gift.

(He takes the package from the minister who has been holding it and presents it to Flora who takes it with a smile.)

And as you and yours shall use this same service at your family board in the new world so may you remember us as we shall ever remember you.

Flora

(In a strong, clear voice.)

We shall remember.

Allan
We shall.
(*The other members of the family add their voices.*)

Flora
We thank you all from the depths of our hearts.
(*She hands the package to Allan.*)

Allan
And we will cherish these.

Flora
Speak for us, Allan.

Allan
(*Hesitating and going ahead.*)
Such kindness and such a welcome, sir, require fitting words, and there are no better words for me to say than these—in your reception we are inspired the more to face the course ahead.
(*Nodding to Flora.*)
You, Flory.

Flora
You say it beautifully, Allan.
(*There is a murmur of approval from the people.*)

Mayor
And now you, ma'am. A few words for us to remember and hand down to our children—
(*With deep sonority.*)
—at this hour when the greatest lady of all Scotland stands before us.
(*Flora shakes her head.*)

VOICES

Yes! Speech, speech!

ALLAN

You must, Flory, they expect it.
(*The scene grows quiet waiting.*)

FLORA

(*Staring ahead of her, and then making an effort to keep her voice from trembling.*)

Only this—that it breaks our hearts to leave this country, but we must go. It's the younger people we must think of now as well as ourselves. And I bid any and all of you who remain to follow after us. There is no opportunity here—this poor land is accursed—accursed.
(*Sadly.*)
And what has cursed it? Blood, the blood of centuries—of wars and killings, of clan against clan, of nation against nation—until the very fields are desolate, homes in ruins, the blight of poverty everywhere. You know that, and that's why we are leaving—after these years of struggle, why we have to leave—to escape the curse that has wrecked our ancient home on yonder hill—where in the time of our fathers three hundred of my clan were slaughtered in cold blood as they had slaughtered others before them. The very voice of the old world's grief is heard there in the lament of those old fisherwomen. May we forget it, forget it all in Carolina where we are going—forget the memory of these, the family hates and blood feuds and savagery in which our people died. Peace is there, peace, and love for one another in that new world. And

if ever in the wisdom of the Almighty we should have to take up arms—which I pray we may not—let it be in the defense of a cause more worthy of our heritage—the cause of our empire, one and whole.

Minister
Amen.
>*(The people applaud. The two soldiers come marching Dan Murchison in through the gate. His hands are bound behind him. The soldiers stop as they see everybody listening to Flora.)*

Flora
For after long years, years of suffering and waste and agony, I know this now—
>*(Her voice strong and vibrant, causing even the flag-bearer to straighten up and hold the flag more proudly.)*

—that only in the union of our people can we attain the greatness that awaits us. And wherever we are, wherever destiny leads us, we must work and build forever for that. And so into the new world we go as pioneers in this great intent. This is the challenge—the Highland call that summons us ahead. And as we grow stronger there, so shall the old world draw strength from us, like a great tree whose roots run far and deep through the earth. Thus shall we see these broken branches of our lives again grow green and the gashes and wounds of our native land heal over. And under that great sheltering tree of empire we shall abide.

Voices
Aye, that's a lass.

Flora
(*Her voice heavy with emotion.*)
—For what way otherwise can life be worthy of those who live it—except as men are measured in a cause as right and true as the best that's in them? And our cause is right. In the deep dead hours of night, in the waking hours of dawn, by the bedside of disease and death—there is a witness in my soul that says it's so—and that cause is the union of all our peoples into one. And in that empire's keeping shall be the glory of the world and the safety of the world. This is our duty and this our dream.

(*She bows her head and the people cheer. Dan lets out a hard high laugh, and the crowd look around at him in astonishment, and then murmur among themselves.*)

Dan
(*His lips trembling in scorn and bitterness.*)
Aye, fine and glorious words, Mistress Flora! And what do they mean?

Mayor
Silence!

Dan
Nothing, nothing.

First Soldier
Move on with him.

Flora
(*Quietly.*)
Dan Murchison.

Dan
(*Mockingly.*)
Our destiny and our dream! Lies and oppression and starvation it is.

Allan
(*Angrily.*)
Whist.

Sandy
(*Coming up to him pleadingly.*)
Air ye out of your head, lad?

Dan
And to all the praise and tears of farewell add my last words black with curses.
(*The people mumble and the mayor glares at him.*)

Mayor
Take him away! Away!

Flora
Wait.

Allan
(*To the first soldier.*)
What's his crime?

First Soldier
He was escaping on the ship from the army—and we nabbed him.

Peggy
He's done nothing wrong, I tell you.

Dan

(*Raging at Peggy.*)

Help me now, is it? You never helped me in the days gone by—all them times I tended your horse and waited on your every whim. And there you go riding by, the sunlight around your head like a dream out of heaven, and the birds singing to you and you whistling back, and me a dog chewing mouldy crusts at your father's back door.

(*Peggy bows her head and turns away.*)

Now—it's all over and ended. And you go forth to your mighty destiny and the making of a new world and me to a stinking prison or a hanging gallows.

(*His voice almost breaking into a cry.*)

—And I'll tell ye now, Peggy MacNeill, God forgive me the hours and the bitter nights I've gnawed my heart out with the thoughts of you and your pretty face burning in the core of my soul like a red-hot flame in hell—go on across the water to your proud sweetheart and marry him, and may—

(*He suddenly stops, his face pale and set and his lips trembling with words unsaid.*)

Minister

(*Aghast.*)

God forgive him.

Dan

(*Murmuring.*)

God—He don't hear the poor man and the beggar—That's what I am—what my father was before me.

(*Angrily.*)

And you talking of poverty—wait till you know it—wait

till you lie in a straw bed with a rope knotted around your guts to ease the tearing emptiness.
(*He starts away, the soldiers following.*)

Flora
(*Stepping in front of him as the soldiers stop him.*)
You were going to America, Dan?

Dan
(*Without looking up.*)
I was.
(*Muttering.*)
I heard a lie told—a man might be free there and have a chance.

Flora
Can't we do something, Allan?
(*Allan is silent.*)

Peggy
Please, Uncle Allan.
(*Dan stares suddenly over at Peggy.*)

Sandy
I got twelve pence I'll lend ye, Dan.

Dan
Thankee, Sandy, but the king deals only in pounds.
(*To the captain in sudden desperation.*)
Would you have a place for the workingest man you've ever seen on the topside of the earth? Would you, sir?

Captain
You're no sailor.

Dan
I'd learn it—I can climb any mast or pole ever made.

Peggy
He can, Captain.

Flora
He could help us, Allan. There are fields to be cleared and buildings. He would help.

Dan
(*Shaking his head.*)
But I'm against you, ma'am, and you all—and against what you stand for. I don't believe in this same king and this same empire you talk about. And why—because it's always been hunger and pain under him.

Flora
You'd learn to believe in them. Then your hot head would be worth the more.

Dan
But I'd work for you, Master Allan, serve my time and fill the place of two men.

Allan
(*To the captain.*)
Will you take him on as a member of your crew for his passage, Captain?

THE HIGHLAND CALL

CAPTAIN

I'd try him—

DAN

A trial is all that I need—
  (*Roaring to the soldiers in sudden joy.*)
You hear that? Untie me!

FIRST SOLDIER

(*Firmly.*)
He's still the king's man. He must be bought free first.

PEGGY

How much is it?

FIRST SOLDIER

Four pound sixpence to hire another in his place, ma'am.

PEGGY

I can furnish it.

ANNE

Peggy!

DAN

Don't worry, Miss Anne—I can't take yonder bridegroom's money—

ALEXANDER MACLEOD

Quiet, will you!

DAN

Ah—

ANNE

Then take him as a bound boy, father—let him sign.

Dan

Aye, and I'd do that gladly—bind myself—put my name on paper, and I'm your man till it's paid.

Allan

(*As he looks at Flora.*)
Agreed.

MacLeod

And I misdoubt not we'll all be sorry for it.

Allan

Eigh?

MacLeod

He will give somebody trouble.

Dan

True, my thoughts will be my own, but my hands will be yours to the last farthing of my debt, sir.

MacLeod

And then?

Flora

You hurry matters, Alec.

Allan

Untie him.
   (*The soldiers free him. At this moment a voice is heard calling off at the right.—"Your excellency! —your excellency—e—ee!" A lad comes running in with a large letter in his hand and gives it to the mayor.*)

Lad

By the post—sir—your honor.
(*The mayor stares at the letter.*)

Mayor

The royal seal!
(*He opens it quickly and looks about him.*)
From his majesty himself.

Voices

The king. You hear that? That paper's from the king.

Mayor

(*Reading in a loud and eager voice.*)
"To my loyal subjects of Campbelltown and Kintyre and to Flora MacDonald and her husband of Kingsboro—greetings—"

Allan

(*With joyous pride.*)
Ah, Flory.
(*She looks up at him and smiles.*)

Mayor

(*Continuing.*)
"Whereas the late master and mistress of Kingsboro in the Isle of Skye have expressed their desire to migrate to America—
(*With a slight change of tone.*)
—will his excellency the mayor of Campbelltown convey to them his majesty's blessing in that desire. They will continue in their sworn fealty to our person and at all

times be zealous in our cause. Therefore let it be known that for their constant and loyal service his majesty doth hereby designate them as persons of warrant and favor to the king and accordingly hath ordered the purchase of a plantation for them out of crown funds upon their arrival in North Carolina. Given this date—"
(The people applaud and Allan puts his arm around Flora. The mayor hands Flora the king's letter and bows.)

YOUNG ALEXANDER AND JAMES
(Throwing up their caps.)
Hooray for the king!

OTHERS
Long live the king!
(Dan turns with a bundle of luggage, then stops as the minister steps forward and lifts his hands in prayer over the assembly.)

MINISTER
Almighty and everlasting God, in whom is the life and the light of man, we commend unto thy keeping these thy servants.

PEOPLE
Blessed be the name of the Lord our God.

MINISTER
Land them safely with peril past and be with them in their great endeavor, for their country and their king, and thine be the glory forever and ever, amen.

THE HIGHLAND CALL

PEOPLE

Amen.

(And now townspeople run up to Flora and her family and kiss their hands saying good-by. Some of the girls cluster around Peggy, whispering to her and weeping. Peggy is weeping also. Dan follows the flag-bearer through the gate. The organ strikes up and all begin to sing as they march away, including the townspeople who remain behind. The chorus in the loge joins in.)

PEOPLE AND CHORUS
(In a great unison.)

> Fareweel, O, fareweel,
> My heart it is sair;
> Fareweel, O, fareweel!
> I'll see him nae mair.
> Lang, lang was he mine,
> Lang, lang, but nae mair,
> I maunna repine,
> But my heart is sair.

(The townspeople crowd against the fence at the left and stare off. They hold their hands in the air waving them and gradually let them fall. In the distance the sound of the captain's huge voice can be heard.)

VOICE

Cast away! Let go!

THE HIGHLAND CALL

OTHER VOICES
(*Exultant and loud.*)
Aye, aye, sir!
(*The singing continues from the distant ship and the chorus, and then dies away. The people gradually lower their heads, and here and there some can be seen wiping their eyes. And now swelling in louder from the left rear comes the keening of the old women. The scene fades out and the light comes up on Mr. Mac in the loge at the right.*)

MR. MAC

And so the great adventure into a new land and a new life began. After weeks of hazardous sailing, the crowded and frail little ship finally arrived at Wilmington, and the town turned out in welcome. Bells were rung, flags fluttered from many a balcony, and the city's single cannon fired off its thundering salute. Many of the MacDonald clan had come down the river to meet their kinsmen. And it was with troubled jealous heart that young Dan Murchison saw Donald MacDonald kiss Peggy MacNeill, his bride-to-be. Ah, but what could he, a bond servant, do about it? Still they were not married yet, thank God for that, and beyond the present he would not think. And as he went about helping unload the ship, he kept the memory of the few words he had spoken to her on the long voyage and the songs he had sung in the nights of his lonely watch hoping she'd hear him. And maybe she had, for they say women have an ear for such things.

The first care was for a home. All reports spoke of the grazing and farm lands up the Cape Fear River high above the fevered swamps and lowlands. And the family loaded their belongings on flatboats and poled themselves

THE HIGHLAND CALL   49

for ten days along the winding stream until they came to the village of Cross Creek, now our town of Fayetteville. Here they resided for a while in a house belonging to old Hugh MacDonald, Flora's stepfather and grandfather of Donald. The foundations of this house can be seen to this day there on the bank of the creek opposite MacNeill's mill. A settlement was temporarily made at what is now Cameron's Hill, some seven or eight miles north of the present Fort Bragg, and there they planted corn, peas, oats, and barley and began the accumulation of a small herd of cattle. Finally they found the place they'd been looking for—among the rolling and watered hills of what is now Richmond County. There with the help of their servants and friends and young Dan Murchison, they set about building a house, a mill-dam, and clearing the fields. At last Flora and Allan MacDonald had reached the haven where they would be, and the years stretched smilingly ahead.

And so there in the wilderness they worked steadily on. Hour after hour, day after day, the sound of their axes, their saws and hammers could be heard in the wilderness, and beam by beam their house shouldered up its sturdy way, there among the pines above a flowing spring.

(*The light dies away from Mr. Mac and comes up on the center stage.*)

SCENE 3

The setting is a pine forest at the foot of a hill, several months later. To the right is a little leafy glade with a spring at the mouth of it. Near the spring is a wash pot with charred embers around it. A few boulders are scattered about and a log lies rotting in the leaves and vines across the left rear. A path at the left leads down the hill and across the scene to the spring. The scene is a rich pattern of autumn colors among the dogwoods, maples and haws—red, purple, orange, brown and light yellow, and the warm rays of the October sun spill through in glowing spots upon the mossy ground. When the curtain rises, Peggy MacNeill is finishing laying out lunch on the slope of the hill from a hamper which sits in the foreground. She makes a beautiful picture with her cap, bright skirt, and red shawl. As she works away she hums to herself against the background noises of hammers and saws in the distance, punctuated now and then by the shout of a man saying, "Hold it. Ease a bit on the end! Let her go!" A bird begins singing from one of the leafy boughs above. Peggy stops and looks up.

Peggy
(*Smiling and puckering her lips in a bird call.*)
Psh-w-ee, wee—wee.

(A moment she listens so, and then lays out a big loaf of bread and begins slicing it with a hunting knife. The knife grows still in her hand and she sits thinking. Gradually her humming rises into abstracted

THE HIGHLAND CALL 51

song as she stares off before her. The organ plays a hushed accompaniment.)

> I wish I were where Helen lies,
> For night and day on me she cries,
> I wish I were where Helen lies,
>   On fair Kirconnel lee.
>
> O Helen fair beyond compare,
> I'll make a garland of thy hair,
> Shall bind my heart forever mair,
>   Until the day I dee.

(*Her voice dies out and she goes on slicing the bread. Sandy's voice is heard calling off at the left.*)

SANDY

Hei-i-g-h, Sime-ee!
(*He comes in, hot and bothered, wearing his old kilt and tam now unashamed. His torn jacket is streaked with sweat and his grizzled face toil-worn and grimy.*)
Ain't seen Simey, ha' ye, Miss Peggy?

PEGGY

No, Sandy.

SANDY

(*Going over to the spring and dipping up a gourdful of water.*)
Ga'dang it, every time my back is turned, skeet and he's gone into them woods again—hunting for Indians.

PEGGY
(*With a light laugh.*)
But he always comes back.

SANDY
(*Dropping the gourd back into the spring and fanning himself.*)
Aye, after I've done broke my back straining at them timbers and him strong as an ox.
(*Sinking down on the ledge of rocks.*)
Ah, Lard, I should a-stayed in Cross Creek there. Master Donald wanted me to be his man, but in my great loyalty to Mistress Flora I riz, bowed, and said, "Master Donald," I says, "by the great sarpent stone, I canna do it. Man and boy we been with the MacDonalds for generations since the first capture in the lowlands, and a man's feet should never outrun his shoes." That's what I said, Mistress Peggy.

PEGGY
We couldn't have done without you here, Sandy.

SANDY
(*Wagging his head.*)
And where will it lead to I don't know—such a mommick and a mixture—Mistress Flora like a little girl with a new doll and me like the dead lice was a-dropping from me.

PEGGY
You know you like this outdoor life, Sandy.

Sandy

No, but I'll serve 'em, like Dan Murchison there, with a great twisting of guts I'll serve 'em. They's something in me that makes me do it. Let Mistress Flora lift but her lily-white hand and I'd brave all the dark varmints and hell cats living in these wildsome woods—
   (*Sighing.*)
Ah, I'm drove hard and put up muddy all my life.

Peggy

Aunt Flora's hands are not so lily-white now, Sandy.

Sandy

And every cut with the axe and blow with the hammer, she says, is helping to build the great empire forever. Fust it was Cross Creek—the town didn't suit. Then it was Mount Pleasant—that weren't fur enough—and now we're out here in this ungodly wilderness a-hacking and a-building, a-shouting and a-calling. Two years ago we sailed on that ship, and it might ha' been a hundred.
   (*His voice dying in a complaining drone.*)
Why I should be in my prime, and here I am knee-deep in the grave.

Peggy

You look better than I've ever seen you, Sandy.

Sandy

Deceiving—deceiving—and all my speed's in the spurs now.
   (*A faint, high halloo comes out of the forest at the right. Sandy springs up, calling.*)

Eigh, Simey! Stand where ye air, boy!
> (*He hurries out at the right front. Peggy stares after him a moment and then goes on arranging the food. The bird begins his song once more in the trees above. Peggy, as if infected by his notes, starts singing again.*)

Peggy
> I wish my grave were growing green,
> A winding sheet o'er both my e'en,
> And I in Helen's arms lying,
> > On fair Kirconnel lee.

(*Dan comes in along the path carrying a heavy armful of wood. He stops behind her.*)

Dan
Please don't stop.

Peggy
> (*Looking up startled.*)

Oh—

Dan
> (*Half-reciting.*)
> > As I came down the mountain side,
> > None but my foe to be my guide,
> > None but my foe to be my guide—

Peggy
You know it.

Dan
Aye.

PEGGY

It's beautiful, sad and beautiful. My mother used to sing it.

DAN

Mine too, and my grandmammy before her.
(*As they are both silent.*)

PEGGY

Don't stand there breaking your back with that great load of wood. Put it down.

DAN

I wasn't thinking of it.
(*He hurries over to the right, drops the wood and begins piling it around the pot.*)
Want me to bring the fire now?

PEGGY

I'll finish the wash after dinner.
(*As he starts away.*)
Why are you in such a hurry?

DAN

I got to get back to work.

PEGGY

(*Looking at the sun.*)
But we're all going to eat now.

DAN

(*A little sharply.*)
Yes, you all are.

Peggy

(*Ignoring the tone of his voice.*)
Sit down and rest awhile, Dan. You're always moving, fetching and carrying.

Dan

They're the terms of my contract—I'll do as much as two men, I said.

Peggy

And you have—nobody can deny that. They're all talking about how hard you work.

Dan

I like to work.

Peggy

Without you, no telling when the house would be finished. Uncle Allan and Aunt Flora are thankful to you.

Dan

I'm glad they're thankful.

Peggy

Can I ask you a question, Dan?

Dan

You can, Mistress Peggy.

Peggy

(*Frankly.*)
Why are you so unhappy?
    (*Dan is silent.*)
You are, you know.

Dan
Then I am if you say so, and I'm not if you say so.

Peggy
(*With a touch of spirit.*)
You needn't poke fun at me—

Dan
I know, it's not good taste—but I've got no taste then. I'm only a servant for Master Allan MacDonald.

Peggy
(*In distress.*)
Dan!—Oh, you're so touchy all the time.

Dan
(*With a slight crude bow.*)
All right then, I am touchy—and a fool with it. God forgive me.

Peggy
God forgive you for what?

Dan
That's just a saying, ain't it?

Peggy
Go ahead—you're always mum as a post. Tell me what bothers you so?

Dan
Why should I?

PEGGY

Because—because I want to hear it. I hate to see you worried all the time.

DAN

A man has to have his thoughts, don't he?

PEGGY

But not such bitter ones as yours seem to be. You were so gay at first—on the ocean, then at Cross Creek. Now in these past months you've grown dark and bitter as a cloud.

DAN

Your eyes are too sharp, ma'am.

PEGGY

Takes no sharp eyes to see that. Hasn't coming to America meant what you thought, Dan?

DAN

It's not what I thought, all right. Oh, but you don't want to bother with me. Your lord has just come there, riding on his fine horse and with his lace and shoes shining in the sun.

PEGGY

Donald?

DAN

Aye. And you soon to be married to him and with slaves and bond servants to wait on you. Maybe you'd give me a job.

(*He starts away, and then turns sharply back.*)

Lies, lies, it all was—

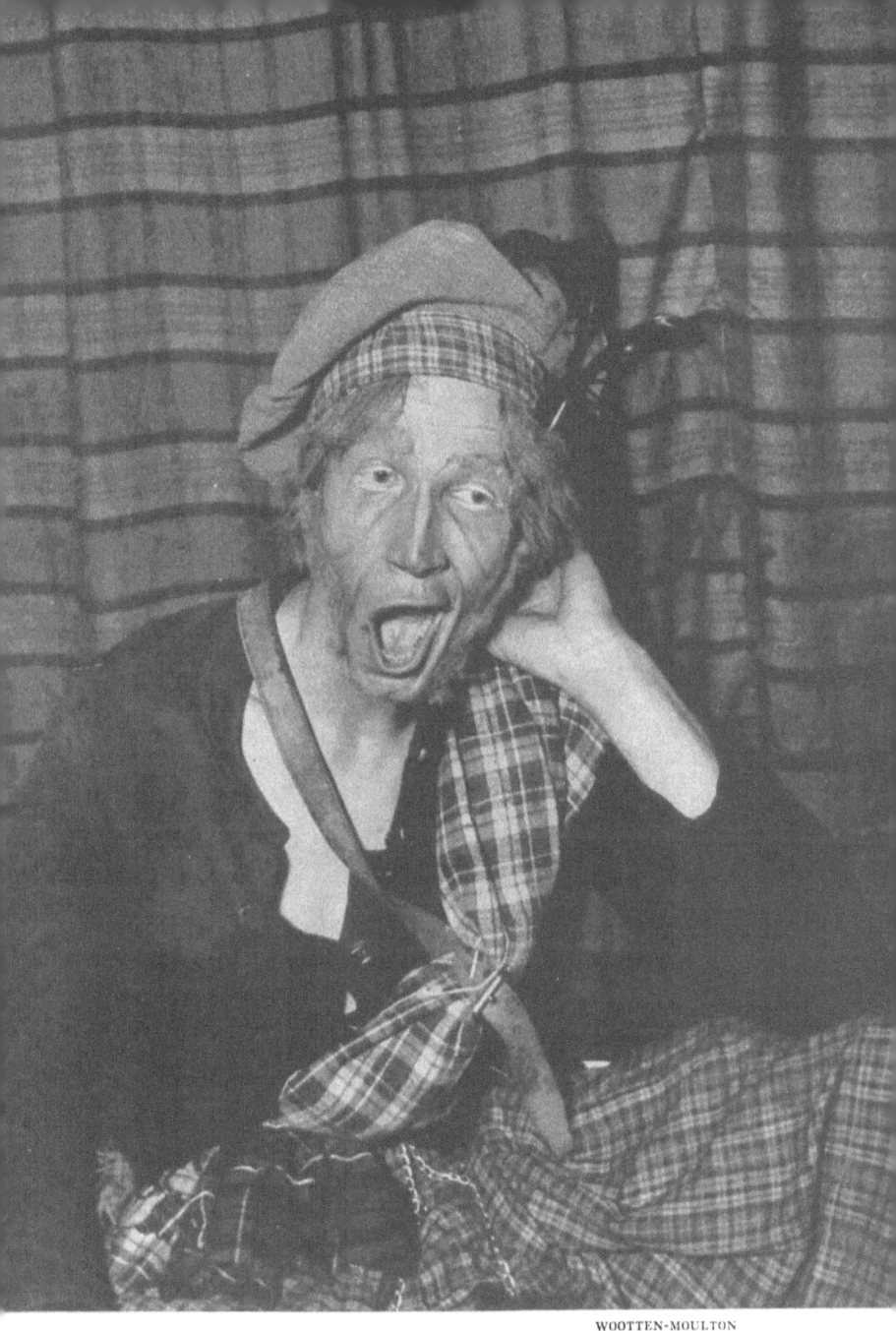

WOOTTEN-MOULTON

SANDY OCHILTREE, of the Clan Ochiltree (*played by Donald Mason*), repents of a full night of drinking

THE MACDONALDS toast their king in the wilds of North Carolina (1939 production)

Peggy

What lies, Dan?

Dan

All they've said about this country. Oh yes, over here a man was a man—and that's all that counted. Through the power of his own hands he could build his own life the way he wanted it. People could be free and there was a chance for everybody. Lies it was, I tell you.

Peggy

And you will have your own life—somehow you will.

Dan

And how—how? I ask you. Don't the same old ways carry on here? The strong and the proud have everything the way they did in Scotland, and the poor must work for the powerful? And it will keep being that way. I see it now.

Peggy

But you have only a few days more to serve your time.

Dan

So you remember it, do you? The rest have forgot it—think I'm theirs forever.

Peggy

I have remembered it, Dan. And then you'll be free.

Dan

Free for what—to get a rifle and hunting knife and tramp the wilderness like Daniel Boone or that poor old Simey

wandering loony in the woods? I—That's not for me. I want my own place—
(*Staring at her hungrily.*)
—my own home—Ah, Peggy MacNeill—
(*Shaking his head.*)
No—I'll go on working here for Master Allan or some other property man—and I'll be his tenant or tend his flocks, and die as I would in Scotland.
(*Peggy is silent, looking before her.*)
And you—you—just the same as it was intended. You'll marry and be a rich merchant's wife there in Cross Creek among your people. And all this singing and laughing and talk about the free air of the great woods out here and how you love it means nothing, nothing.

Peggy

I do love it here, Dan. I've never been so happy before—that's the truth.

Dan

And so that's how it is—the new land is the old land, and the new people are the old people as they've always been—greedy and grasping. And there in the great books in the courthouse they sign themselves over to the control of things, and fellows at the bottom like me stay—at the bottom.

Peggy

That's unfair, and you know it. Why, Uncle Allan and Aunt Flora would do all they could to help you get started. They'll help you get a grant of land—they will.

Dan

And still they'd be the great MacDonalds and I'd be Dan Murchison, and you—you are still one of the great Mac-

Neills, high and proud like God Almighty, and you will be till the end of time.
(*Suddenly grinding his fists together.*)
And you ask me about my bitter thoughts. Ah, God, sometimes I hate them, hate you—all of you.

Peggy

Dan—

Dan

And night and day it eats in me like a bile bitter as death, and I feel like crying out—reaching out with my two hands and strangling something, whatever it is that holds me down, to crush it, stamp on it, and stand above it all a free man, free as this wilderness that reaches from here to the mountains and beyond.
(*Hopelessly.*)
But there's no chance—like my poor father there in Scotland. I know it now.

Peggy

(*Staring at him with flushed cheek.*)
At last you tell me what you're thinking. Thank you for that.

Dan

And what do you care? Once there on the wharf when I was lightheaded with starvation I told you how I'd dreamed about you—hah, hah—told you how I'd worshipped you—looking up to you like a star in the sky, and in my crazy mind I'd dreamed of the day in this new world when I'd have the power to touch that star, aye, to pluck it down and put it in my bosom here—like it might ease me.

(*Peggy looks at him.*)

And what did I find here—the same old pride and power of the clan, except worse, and everywhere the arm of the king and the glory of England over us. So it was all lies, lies, I tell you.

(*Donald MacDonald enters suddenly down the path and into the scene. He is about twenty-five years old, of medium height, and with a quick tongue and restless hands. In contrast to Dan he is well dressed, with a show of lace at his throat and wrists.*)

Donald

(*As he enters.*)
What lies, young fellow?

Peggy

(*Springing up.*)
Why, Donald—when did you come?

Donald

Just a moment back.
(*To Dan.*)
What's your name?

Dan

Dan Murchison.

Donald

Oh—the bound boy—I remember now—and still the growling and complaining.

Dan

Aye, that's the one privilege I've got.

Donald

And, by God, why are you standing talking to Miss Peggy here like her equal? Take off your cap.

Peggy

Donald.

Dan

I like it where it is.

Donald

(*Angrily.*)
Get out. Go up the hill there and tend to my horse. Give him plenty of hay and oats. He's had a hard trip.
(*To Peggy.*)
I was so anxious to get here—
(*As Dan does not move.*)
You hear me?

Dan

Yes.

Donald

Then do as you are told.

Dan

It's true I obey orders, but not yours.

Donald

(*Incredulously.*)
What!

(*Raising his riding crop.*)
I should thrash you for this.
(*He starts towards Dan.*)

PEGGY

(*Running between them.*)
Stop it, Donald!

DONALD

(*Stuttering with rage.*)
My God—who does he think he is!

PEGGY

Go on, please, Dan.
(*Dan turns and goes up the hill.*)
Come on, sit down. We're going to have dinner right away.

DONALD

(*Staring after Dan.*)
Is that fellow crazy? I could kill him for that.

PEGGY

Don't think about it. Tell me the news in Cross Creek. How is old Cousin Hugh? Here, taste some of these muscadines. I gathered them this morning. The woods are full of them.
(*She lifts a small basket to him.*)

DONALD

No, thank you.
(*Shaking his head in thought.*)
You know, Peggy, there's something queer happening in this country. Over in town the riffraff are beginning to act

like that fellow—insolent to their superiors. I don't understand it.

PEGGY

Sometimes I think maybe—

DONALD

And there's only one way to deal with it—force. Ah, my sweet, but we'll forget that now.
  (*Turning, he puts his arm around her and kisses her cheek.*)
And how are you?

PEGGY

(*Moving around and arranging the food.*)
Well—oh, I'm fine.

DONALD

You've never looked more beautiful. And I have the news you've waited to hear. The house is finished.

PEGGY

Finished.

DONALD

The carpenters are putting on the last touches. I've hurried it up. Two nights ago I walked through the empty rooms and thought—only another week and you'd be there. The furniture is in.

PEGGY

You've worked hard, Donald.

DONALD

I have. And you'll be the queen of the town. Kiss me.

Peggy

They're coming.

Donald

(*Looking off.*)
It's nobody but Sandy.
(*He hugs her to him.*)
The Reverend Mr. MacLeod's coming down from Barbecue Church for the ceremony. Everything is arranged for next Tuesday—
(*Peggy says nothing.*)
—the day of the festival in town. Crowds of people will be there—games and foot races, and a tournament. I'm to ride in it, and I'll wear your colors. I'll win the prize for you too.

Peggy

(*Looking at him.*)
You love me, don't you?

Donald

And who wouldn't—you the bonniest lass that ever crossed the ocean?
(*He hums a verse of song as he sits down and watches her admiringly. Sandy comes in muttering to himself.*)
Greetings, Sandy.

Sandy

(*Bowing and scraping to him.*)
And how are ye, Master Donald?
(*Shaking his head in wonder.*)
Lord, you look fresh as a new piece of money. Don't he, Miss Peggy?

Peggy

He does, Sandy.

Donald

And how are ye, Sandy?

Sandy

Nohow, sir, nohow.
   (*Sharply.*)
And it's on account of work—a short and simple word, Master Donald, but you might search a month of Sundays to find one with a nastier meaning in it.
   (*He limps over to the spring again, lifts out a gourdful of water and drinks it.*)

Peggy

We've all been working, Donald.
   (*Stretching out her hands, palms upward.*)
See my hands.

Donald

   (*Blowing her a kiss.*)
But you won't have to do any more of that.

Peggy

Oh, but I've liked it. Yesterday I even milked a cow.

Sandy

   (*Wagging his head.*)
That I should have ever lived to see it—and she with kings and lords in her family stretching back to Noah.

Peggy
But I'm forgetting all that—
  (*Staring off and echoing.*)
—out here I am.

Sandy
Oh, they ain't no telling what corruption will come upon a body in this wild land. Yea, I'm totally destroyed with the labor they've piled upon my poor bent shoulders.
  (*He eases himself down grunting on the ground.*)
It's "Sandy the hogs need feeding," and "Sandy, there's a sick cow a mile beyond the creek." And "Sandy, hold this beam," and "Sandy, run down the hill and fetch up a pail of water." Ah, praise the Lord that there house is about finished. And such a house, Master Donald. All the tempest and floods and power of the elements won't move it. Them foundations they've put down will last beyond the day of doom.

Donald
And how is Simey faring out here?

Sandy
Mad as a fish—Indian mad—dreams about 'em all the time—hunts for 'em in the woods and leaves the work to me.

Donald
You must come over and stay with Mistress Peggy and me.

Sandy
Aye, and maybe I can rest a bit. I tell you, if I'd a-known what taming this wilderness was to be I'd a-kept myself

THE HIGHLAND CALL

safe in Scotland and died there with Simey. Ochon—ochrie. There's no time for anything here but work, work, work—chop, chop, chop. And that young terror in the shape of mortal man up at the glim of dawn hacking away so nobody can sleep. It's him, Master Donald, that leads us into these doleful doings.

DONALD
Who?

SANDY
That Dan Murchison. They said we'd have trouble with him over here, and we have. He's a plumb devil on wheels. And there's no time for fun any more. I ain't had a note out of my instermint in a month.

PEGGY
But in a few days we'll all be moved in and the winter rains will fall. Then you can rest.
(A noise is heard in the woods at the right again—now like the low whine of a dog.)

SANDY
Dad-dum it, that's him again.
(Getting to his feet and calling.)
Cooshy—cooshy—coo. We ain't going to hurt you, Simey.
(A plaintive call comes back from the woods.)
Maybe I can tole him.
(He gets some food in his hand and goes away at the right.)

DONALD
And now let me tell you another surprise—Governor

Martin may be at our wedding. I sent a special invitation...

Peggy
I've forgot the goblets.
(*Flora and Allan MacDonald come in. They are dressed much as before, but both show signs of rough outdoor work.*)

Allan
You young folks got everything talked over?

Donald
Pretty much so.

Flora
Have we plenty to eat, Peggy? Cousin Alec will dine with us.

Allan
Colonel Alexander MacAllister from Barmore in the Bluff section. You know him, Donald.

Donald
I do—a notorious old Whig and as full of treason as an adder.

Flora
But still our kinsman.

Donald
He's going up and down the land making speeches against the government—I guess you didn't know that.

Flora
Cousin Alec always was one for speeches. There's no harm in him.

Donald
But there's harm in those that listen to him.

Allan
(*In his easygoing way.*)
Cousin Jennie Bhan will keep him quiet.

Donald
And she's another one that'll bear watching. She talks loyal, but wait till a war comes.

Flora
There's no war coming, Donald. Rumors of trouble have been in this country since the Stamp Act in '65. They're nothing but rumors and neighborhood fights. They'll pass. And it's our duty, Donald, to keep a clear head in such things.

Donald
It's the duty of loyal citizens to keep a strong hand on everything. And everybody's not doing it.
(*Calling after Peggy who has started up the path.*)
Wait, Peggy.
(*He goes after her.*)

Allan
(*Gazing after them.*)
They make a likely couple.

FLORA

And I pray a happy one.
> (*They are silent a moment.*)

ALLAN

Look at our house up there, Flory, shining in the sun.

FLORA

It's beautiful—I feel I know every tree that's gone into it. Like being surrounded by friends it'll seem.

ALLAN

And we've chosen the right name for it—Killiegrey.

FLORA

> (*Murmuring.*)

Love's haven—And may it ever be that to us and to our friends and neighbors in the days to come.

ALLAN

> (*Putting his arm around her.*)

It will—We'll make it so. After all these years of trouble and suffering—here in America we'll make it so.

FLORA

Yes, working and building and leading the way on in this great country—you and I.
> (*She sinks down on the boulder.*)

I want to talk with you a minute, Allan, before the others come—about Dan Murchison.

ALLAN

What is it?

Flora

(*Quietly.*)
He's in love with Peggy.

Allan

What!

Flora

She must be sent away with Donald tomorrow.

Allan

Then Dan's daft—out of his mind!

Flora

He's in love.

Allan

The fool. Still he's a wonder of a lad, he is—It's not true, Flory.

Flora

Haven't you seen it, Allan? He's eating his heart out, and all the labor in the world won't ease it. Peggy must be married to Donald and the quicker the better. We've got to see to that.

Allan

Ah, he's already planned it at the festival. She don't seem so—
(*Suddenly starting.*)
My Lord!

Flora

Now you've thought of that too.

ALLAN
It's impossible. Peggy wouldn't.

FLORA
It's not impossible. We've let down the barriers here maybe too much—all busy together. And if time went by and she stayed here she might forget her pride and—
(Her voice dies out.)

ALLAN
(Muttering.)
Then she'd be daft as he is.

FLORA
It would be tragic. Such things don't work. For a short while in the hot blood of youth—then they'd have to face the truth—he a bond servant and she a MacNeill of Barra.

ALLAN
She's given her plighted word to Donald long ago, and would never break it.

FLORA
No, but she could break her heart. We must see them married at once.
(Allan's reply is swallowed up by the sound of running footsteps. Alexander MacDonald comes flying in, pursued by his brother James. They race by the spread-out food and over to the spring where a good-natured scuffle takes place.)

JAMES
I win.

Jennie Bhan MacNeill (*played by Josephine Sharkey*) berates Colonel MacAllister (*played by Allan Frank*) for his political views

The Cape Fear Highlanders (1939 production) honor Flora MacDonald (played by Margaret Holmes) with the Highland Fling (danced by the Flora MacDonald College girls)

WOOTTEN-MOULTON

Alexander
No, you don't.

James
I touched you.

Alexander
(*Drinking from the gourd and turning to Allan.*)
I leave it to you, father—which won?

James
(*Gulping down a drink.*)
I did.

Alexander
(*Coming over to the food and getting a handful.*)
I bet him my hunting knife I'd peg my course of boards first.

James
I finished quick as he did.

Alexander
And then I beat him to the spring.

James
I touched him first.

Allan
I declare it a dead heat.

Alexander
(*Disgustedly, his mouth full of food.*)
All right, he's the baby.
  (*James comes over and reaches himself some food.*)

Flora
You might wait a moment for the others, Jamie.

Allan
(*With pride in his voice.*)
Don't you young men get enough work to do without running wild over the place?

Alexander
That's not work—it's fun.

James
I hope we'll build another house right away.

Allan
And what about those law books?

James
Uhm—

Allan
And the Reverend MacLeod is expecting you, Alec, in two weeks.

Alexander
I've been thinking about this preaching matter, Father.

Allan
Well, that's dutiful, it needs thought, prayerful thought.

Alexander
I mean—
(A chatter of voices is heard off at the left, and Colonel Alexander MacAllister, Jennie Bhan MacNeill, Donald and Peggy come in. Peggy is bearing several silver goblets on a tray. Colonel MacAllister is a heavy, imposing Scotchman about sixty-five years old, and voluble as to words and gestures. He is well dressed and wears his gray hair long on his temples. Jennie Bhan is about sixty years old, a rough peppery woman, with square features, and as square brogan shoes—a person of great heart and ability.)

Jennie Bhan
(As they enter.)
And I'll say this again, Alec MacAllister, we need your working hands more than your talking tongue.

Allan
What's the trouble, Cousin Jennie Bhan?

Jennie Bhan
Alec's come over here to make us a political speech, I can tell it by the droop of his mouth.

MacAllister
Ah, but my heart sunk in me, Jennie, when I saw you. I knew there'd be no chance for it.

Jennie Bhan
I hope not.

MacAllister
Ahm—
   (*Nodding.*)
My respects to you, Donald.

Donald
   (*Coldly.*)
Thank you.

MacAllister
So—by that tone you're not pleased to see me either.

Donald
I don't like your politics, Cousin Alec, and you know it.

Jennie Bhan
Let's eat now and argue later.

Alexander
I say so.

James
And I.

MacAllister
You've got two fine boys here, Allan.

Allan
They'll do in a pinch.

MacAllister
When are you sending over for the other children, Flory?

Flora
Soon now, we hope.

MacAllister
I wouldn't do that—not yet.

Allan
Why not?

MacAllister
Because of the trouble—No, we said we'd eat first.
   (*Surveying the food.*)
Uhm—Did you fix this dinner, Peggy?

Peggy
Part of it.

James
Aw, she did it all by herself.

Jennie Bhan
That's a sensible lass.
   (*She reaches down and gets an apple, then spits off to one side.*)

Donald
After this week she'll have her own cook—two of 'em.

Jennie Bhan
No doubt. They say you're getting rich as river mud, Donald—on slaves and tar and turpentine.

Donald
(*With a glint in his eye.*)
I'm doing right well, thank you, and I've got a branch store going up at Averysboro.

Jennie Bhan
And I hope there ain't any porch on it where Cousin Alec can address the crowd.

Donald
If there is I'll take it off.
(*Dan Murchison comes in at the left rear with a jug. He stops and waits.*)

Jennie Bhan
Uhm—what apples.
(*She takes a bite like a horse.*)

Flora
Anne sent them to us from Glendale. And that wine too. Pour it around, Dan.
(*Peggy passes the goblets among them and Dan goes about pouring.*)

MacAllister
(*As Jennie Bhan chews away.*)
Be careful, Cousin Jennie, you'll break out that one tooth.

Jennie Bhan
Now you're throwing off on me **again**. And didn't the blacksmith tell me Monday a week ago I had the finest set of teeth he'd ever seen—on a woman of my age. And Ben Franklin himself bragged on 'em once. Ah, that was a lad.

MacAllister
I forgive Ben Franklin the lie—
  (*Looking about him.*)
For he's one of the leaders in the Whig cause.

Jennie Bhan
(*Sputtering.*)
You old trouble-maker, you could have talked all day and not said that word.

Flora
The blessing please, Cousin Alec.
  (*They all bow their heads.*)

MacAllister
(*Hesitating and then intoning.*)
Our heavenly Father, we bow our heads in thanksgiving before thee. Bless us and bless this food to thy name's honor and glory. Be with us in the hours and days to come —times perhaps fraught with sorrow and struggle. Teach us to stand together as friends and neighbors and kinsmen for the cause of truth—a cause that may be tested sooner than—
  (*Jennie clears her throat loudly.*)
—sooner than—
  (*Shortly.*)
Amen.

Several of the Others
Amen.

DONALD
(Lifting his glass.)
And now a word to you all—
> *(Peggy bends suddenly down and lifts a plate of food from the ground.)*

PEGGY
Some roast, Cousin Jennie.
> *(Sandy comes backing into the scene from the left with his bread-filled hand extended in front of him. A ragged and piteous Simey is following him.)*

SANDY
(Calling sweetly.)
Cooshy—cooshy—coo. Don't notice him, folkses. I'm trying to get him up the hill and put him in the stable.
> *(They all watch him.)*

JENNIE BHAN
And you better wash him.

JAMES
Sandy's got him this time.

ALEXANDER
Now maybe he'll stop grunting in the woods at night.

SANDY
(Wheedling.)
Cooshy—cooshy—coo—Come on, Simey.
> *(He backs out at the left rear, Simey still following hungrily.)*

Flora
Donald has something to say.

Donald
(*As they all grow still.*)
This—Peggy and I are to be married next week.
> (*Dan stands without a sign to show that he has heard, while the others applaud. Alexander and James slap Donald on the back. There are ad-lib. expressions of "So, it's all fixed up at last," "Good," "Bravo," etc.*)

Allan
We drink to them.
> (*They lift their goblets and drink.*)

Donald
And everybody's invited to Cross Creek next Tuesday.

Jennie Bhan
Half the girls in Cumberland County are sick with envy, Peggy.

Allan
Some more wine.
> (*They hold their goblets out and Dan pours.*)

This good news makes us all glad. And now our toast— Flory—on this special day.

Flora
Even in the wilderness, Cousin Alec, we do not forget.
> (*Colonel MacAllister says nothing as she continues, holding her glass aloft, the others doing likewise.*)

At this hour our hearts turn again to him who reigns over

us. Though separated by three thousand miles of treacherous ocean, there is no separation in our hearts.

Donald
(*Fervently.*)
And shall never be.

Flora
United in spirit, united in purpose, we continue in our loyal devotion to him—Long live the king!

Others
Long live the king!
(*With the exception of Colonel MacAllister and Dan, they all lift their goblets with reverence, though Peggy seems a little slow in raising hers.*)

MacAllister
(*With sudden loudness.*)
You're blind—all of you are blind as bats. Here in the wilderness drinking and toasting a figurehead that has no meaning any more.

Jennie Bhan
Eat, everybody, eat and don't listen to him.
(*She dives in, followed by Alexander and James.*)

MacAllister
I'll have my say, I will, and it's for your sake, Flory and Allan, I'm telling you. I've come over here to ask you to join in our cause.

Flora
There's only one cause to serve. We're doing that, and—in peace.

MacAllister
Listen to me—you—all of you. A struggle is beginning in this country against your king and parliament and—

Flora
Your king also.

MacAllister
He's not mine—

Donald
Then you are a traitor, by God.

MacAllister
And you, young squirt, are a fool and blinded like the rest.
   (*Donald controls his anger by dashing down the rest of his wine.*)

Allan
But scattered colonies like these can never raise a rebellion against the power of the empire.

MacAllister
But they're doing that very thing—and why? For their liberty and rights.

Flora
It's not liberty but license you're talking about. And when the time comes that every Tom, Dick, and Harry can cry out this liberty and rights, then you've got no government

—nothing but mutual fights and killings. We learned that in the clan wars in Scotland. And we learned it well.

(*With sudden energy.*)

If the authority of the king were taken away, these colonies like children would start quarrelling among themselves. There'd be civil wars and blood feuds from Maine woods to Florida. You know that.

MACALLISTER

They'd learn to govern themselves.

FLORA

It's never been done.

MACALLISTER

(*Earnestly.*)

You and Allan are persons of note, Flory, wards as it were of the king, and when trouble breaks out you will be in danger. This thing will spread like a great forest fire, and the tallest trees will make the biggest blaze. You've got to declare yourselves for our cause. Then you'd be safe.

ALLAN

(*With a touch of anger.*)

And break our sacred oath?—Never.

FLORA

It's not only the oath we would break, but the very principles we believe in.

JENNIE BHAN

Old Alec's got no principle, Flora. He don't understand you.

MACALLISTER
When I first came over here thirty years ago I believed the way you did. And then gradually something—I don't know what it was—something in this wilderness and the struggle to tame it that gives men a feeling of self-reliance, of—

DONALD
Yes, liberty, we know the word.

MACALLISTER
Liberty. And every man gets the urge to be his own master, to go and come as he pleases, to worship as he pleases. He resents the meddling of parliament and the king and wants to have his own government, something he has created and has a voice in.

FLORA
And the people here have their own government, their assemblies and houses of burgesses, guaranteed by the crown.

MACALLISTER
And all of them controlled by the royal governors under the king—to be dismissed, to be called, to be instructed as they see fit. Oh, I've seen it all happening under my very eyes. My own bond servants caught this new spirit. I freed every one of 'em and helped them get their own start. And they are standing with us to a man.

ALEXANDER
(*To James, softly.*)
Come on.
(*They move off at the left, with their hands full of food.*)

Donald
(Vehemently.)
If we have war, we'll all be in it, and Cousin Flora and Cousin Allan will lead the Clan MacDonald to victory against the rabble of servants and discontented rogues. Bang go our guns, and they scatter to hide in the ditches and fence jambs like the Regulators at Alamance.

MacAllister
You've got a sad awakening ahead of you. This country's going to separate itself from Britain as sure as there's a God in heaven. It's already started—like a crack across an ice pond when the weight's too heavy, and it's widening, widening. Everywhere up and down the land the workers, servants, the poor people are banding themselves together in a common ideal. Poles and banners are being set up in the towns, and the Sons and Daughters of Liberty are organizing and arming themselves. Call them riffraff if you will, but they shoot straight. You all are my kinsmen and I don't want to see you killed.
(Suddenly to Dan.)
I ask you—am I right?
(Dan says nothing but stares at the ground.)
You're a servant—what do you think?

Donald
Aye, he knows better than to speak.

Flora
Give over this mad talk, Cousin Alec. We are all borrowing worry and trouble for nothing. You can clear away, Dan.

Dan

(*Lifting his head.*)

Standing here listening to him talk seems like I begin to see things ahead of me—things I'd never been able to see before.

MacAllister

(*Triumphantly.*)

Hah-hah, what did I tell you?

Allan

You can go back to work, Dan.

Dan

(*Shaking his head.*)

I hear you, Master Allan—today I do. But if a war comes and it's a fight between the powerful that have everything and them that have little or nothing, you know which side I'll take.

(*Crying out suddenly.*)

Maybe that's it—Yes—!

(*With sudden loudness.*)

Against my enemies everywhere—against all that keeps me down. I'd break my way through, push on, stand there somehow a free man and rid of this galling slavery forever—

(*Striking his breast.*)

Free here inside myself.

Allan

(*Anger sweeping his great frame.*)

Silence!

MacAllister

Hah—and there are thousands like him, Allan, I'm warning you.

Donald

(*Fiercely.*)
Thrash him—
(*He lifts his crop.*)

Allan

(*Waving Donald aside.*)
Dan Murchison, you forget your place. Leave us.
(*To the others.*)
I apologize.

Dan

(*Who has been gripped in his own thinking, striking his hands together.*)
Maybe that's it—what he said—
(*Looking over at Peggy with burning eyes.*)
—a new day ahead—a man free—
(*Struggling with his thoughts.*)
—full and equal, and nobody high like a lord and nobody low like a dog—Ah, Peggy MacNeill—then—

Donald

(*Springing in front of him and raising his crop.*)
This time I'll—
(*As Dan looks at him he gradually lowers his hand.*)
No, if there's a war I'll have the pleasure of killing him honorably.
(*Alexander and James come hurriedly in.*)

THE HIGHLAND CALL

JAMES
(*Excitedly.*)
A British officer is here, Father, to see you and Mother.

ALEXANDER
And it's great news.

FLORA
(*In alarm.*)
What's happened?

JAMES
Something about the people being called and we're all to go.

ALEXANDER
At once.
> (*Dan is now piling dishes into the hamper. Allan starts sternly over to him as Colonel Cotton comes striding in. He is a tall British officer, dressed in full uniform. He stops, clicks his heels and salutes. Donald who has sprung up salutes sharply back.*)

COLONEL COTTON
Ah, Lieutenant MacDonald.
> (*He strides over and shakes hands with Donald.*)

DONALD
(*Indicating.*)
My aunt, Flora MacDonald, my Uncle Allan, Cousin Jennie Bhan MacNeill, Colonel MacAllister—
> (*Colonel Cotton bows again.*)

And—my fiancée, Peggy MacNeill.

COLONEL COTTON
(*After a bow to Peggy.*)
I bring greetings from his excellency, the governor
North Carolina and through him his majesty. You,
and you, madam, are called upon to meet with the lc
servants of the king in Cross Creek.
(*Looking about him.*)
Are you all loyal people here?

COLONEL MACALLISTER
Aye, loyal to our belief.

COLONEL COTTON
(*To Dan.*)
Who are you?

ALLAN
One of our servants, sir.

COLONEL COTTON
Um—
(*To Colonel MacAllister.*)
And what do you mean by your remarks, sir?
(*Then, his face changing.*)
Oh, Colonel MacAllister from Barmore.

COLONEL MACALLISTER
The same.

COLONEL COTTON
Then I need not ask are you loyal.

COLONEL MACALLISTER
You need not.

THE HIGHLAND CALL

COLONEL COTTON
(*To Jennie Bhan.*)
And you madam. Are you the king's woman?

JENNIE BHAN
(*Spitting slyly.*)
I am, as you might say, generally speaking.

COLONEL COTTON
Then my words are only for the loyal ones present. Governor Martin has called upon all the clans to meet at Cross Creek Tuesday.

FLORA
And the purpose?

COLONEL COTTON
To consider raising a Highland regiment.

FLORA
But there is no war.

COLONEL COTTON
To raise a regiment to keep the peace as it needs to be kept. And you, madam, are most specially called for to speak to the people.
(*Bowing.*)
Because of your great influence.—And you will be honored.

FLORA
I seek no honor.

Cotton

And you will honor us.
(Firmly.)
It is needful that these orders be obeyed.
(Tapping a document in his hand.)
They are issued in the king's name.

Allan

Then we must go, Flory.

James

Hooray!

Flora

(Her voice almost a cry.)
We want nothing of these troubles, sir.

Cotton

There are no troubles, madam, and it is to prevent them coming that we must show our strength and authority. It need not distress you. The gathering will be in holiday mood of the festival.
(Saluting.)
Tuesday then—

Allan

But you will spend the night here.

Cotton

I must return immediately.
(To Colonel MacAllister.)
I trust, sir, you will take this matter to heart and advise your people wisely.

MACALLISTER
It's not my neighbors that need advice, but the folks here.

COTTON
As you prefer—
(*He salutes again and goes quickly away.*)

ALLAN
We must get our horses ready. You—boys.
(*Alexander and James hurry out.*)

DONALD
Ah, and you'll all be there for the ceremony. Let's hurry and pack, Peggy.

MACALLISTER
And I must ride back to Bluff tonight.

FLORA
Cousin Alec, I plead with you—use your influence with the people.

MACALLISTER
And once more I plead with you to join our cause.

FLORA
Never—I tell you—Everything would be lost then.

ALLAN
We must hurry, Flory.

FLORA
Yes, we will go to Cross Creek, Allan, go and use whatever voice we have to keep us all at peace.

ALLAN
Dan, I'll forget your behavior for the present. Keep the men working until we return.

DAN
(*Lifting the hamper up.*)
Two more days I will, sir.

ALLAN
What!

PEGGY
His service is ended then.

ALLAN
(*After a moment.*)
You'll stay on with us.

DAN
No, sir.

ALLAN
(*Exasperated.*)
But what will you do?

DAN
(*Indicating Colonel MacAllister.*)
If he's right—I know what I'll do.

MACALLISTER
(*With a smile.*)
We'll see you in Cross Creek.

ALLAN
(Throwing up his hands angrily.)
Come.
(They all start up the hill. The organ sounds a flourish of chords. The scene fades out, and the lights come on in the theater.)

INTERMISSION

ACT TWO

SCENE 1

After the intermission, the organist in the loge at the left begins playing the overture. He plays a short introduction of heavy-treaded chords first, and then follows with a light Highland Fling melody. After this he passes into a rephrasing of "The Highland Widow's Lament" and then into the tripping schottische of "Polwart on the Green." The finale leads into a favorite old folksong. In the meantime the chorus has filed into the pit and the lights have gone down to half-dim in the theater. At the end of the overture the lights die out and come up on the chorus as it sits and hums in a deep-throated wordless harmony, "By Yon Bonnie Banks." When the humming concludes, the lights die from the chorus and come up on Mr. Mac standing by his lectern in the loge at the right.

Mr. Mac
(*With his quiet genial smile.*)
I like that old song, and I hope you do. And I hope you'll learn to sing it and many of the others you are hearing here tonight. Our people used to sing them—they made them and they sang them. And let us keep them in our remembrance—keep a song on our lips and a tune in our hearts.
(*Half-singing in his eldish voice.*)
"And ye'll take the highroad and I'll take the lowroad—"
Yes, some of us take one road and some another, and that makes all the difference, doesn't it? And when one

THE HIGHLAND CALL

takes the road he thinks is right, he usually says the road the other fellow takes is wrong. So it was with the people in this valley long ago. They took two opposing views on the question of government—whether the state is supreme or whether the individual is. And as to the results—let the play decide.

(*In a more matter-of-fact tone.*)
In obedience to the governor's summons the MacDonald family arrived at Cross Creek a few days after the preceding scene. The night of their arrival a banquet was held in the old state house a few hundred yards east of where we are at this hour, and many of the Highland leaders of the section were in attendance to honor Flora and her husband Allan, and to celebrate the coming wedding of Donald MacDonald and Peggy MacNeill. The following day was to be the time of the great festival and demonstration of the Highlanders, and already on the different roads that led into Cross Creek—up from the direction of Wilmington, over from Lumberton, down from Bluff and Upper Little River, from Corinth and Jonesboro—the Highlanders were driving through the night on their carts or riding their horses or many of them walking—converging upon the town.

Alarmed by the calling of the clans, Richard Caswell, Cornelius Harnett, and Colonel MacAllister had begun to assemble the Whigs at different points along the valley to be ready in case of trouble. And Dan Murchison had, as soon as his indenture was up, made his way east to the Bluff section and there put himself under the orders of Colonel MacAllister and Robert Rowan, a devoted Whig who lived in this town and was the leader of the boys of Liberty Point. In the few intervening days Dan had become one of their most trusted messengers. And as he rode from crossroad to hamlet, even where the loyalists were thickest, meeting with different groups and hearing their discussions, he more and more understood the cause he was set to follow. For the first time he learned of happenings in the north—of the fiery zeal of Patrick Henry, of Washington and Jefferson and the Adamses in Boston, of the Continental Congress and the momentous questions being debated there, of battles already fought with the British, and the gradual but sure movement among the people everywhere for the creation of their own government and insurance of their rights as free men.

But ever as he rode his lonely journey, the brighter shone the face of Peggy MacNeill within his mind, the fiercer burned her image in his heart. Ah, but what would any of it be worth without her? Tomorrow she would be married and lost to him forever, unless—But what could he do?—he homeless as a dog and with not a stick or stone to call his own? And on this particular night as he rides into the edge of Cross Creek to bring a message to Robert Rowan from Cornelius Harnett, he carries on the long woeful puzzling within himself. Passing along the creek by Cool Spring, he can hear the cheering in the state house where the loyalist leaders are gathered and where toasts are being drunk to Flora MacDonald and her husband, and to Donald MacDonald and Peggy MacNeill.

(*The light dies from Mr. Mac and comes up on the center stage, revealing a garden scene somewhat dimly lit and showing in the back the windows and arches of the state house. A little paling fence with a gate at the left rear crosses the middle background, and at the right front is a seat, with the branch of a tree hanging over it above. A piece or two of shrubbery is set along the fence near the gate. Much*

THE HIGHLAND CALL

of the light that trickles into the scene comes from candles lighted in the houses off to the right and left of the street. When the curtain rises the figure of a poorly dressed young workingman is seen standing at the rear close against the state house. He apparently is listening to what is going on inside, where ever and anon the sound of cheering and applause is heard. A moment passes and then off to the right rear a bell is heard, much like a small dinner bell. Immediately the young workman begins a spieling chant.)

Workman

Sale tomorrow — sale — goods at half-price — distilled spirits—molasses, Madeira wine, beer, ale and porter in bottles—sugar, malt and loaf and brown—coffee and cocoa—candles of tallow and wax and spermaceti—cheese and soap and boots and slippers—
   (The night watchman comes in carrying a lantern. He is a middle-aged heavy-set fellow with a high voice.)

Watchman

Ten o'clock and all is well—
   (To the workman.)
Who are you?

Workman

Master Donald MacDonald's clerk—

Watchman

Ahm—but don't be so loud with your calling.

Workman
I am set to call his wares in the four quarters of the town.

Watchman
Best not disturb the great folks in there.
>   (*He gestures towards the state house with his thumb.*)

Workman
Master MacDonald won't mind—if it brings him a penny.

Watchman
Hah-hah.
>   (*Raising his voice.*)

Ten o'clock and all is well.—God save his majesty the king!
>   (*He goes on out at the left rear ringing his bell.*)

Workman
>   (*Calling again.*)

Pack thread and nails and spikes, salt and tobacco, snuff and indigo, pickled fish and dried fish—saddles, gloves and leather—and—herbs of all kinds bought and sold—
>   (*His voice dies out and after looking carefully about him, he turns back to his listening at the window. Again the sound of applause and cheering is heard within. Dan Murchison comes in at the left rear. He is splashed with mud from long riding. The workman looks up and again starts his spiel.*)

Wrought pins, pewterware and glasses—black bottles, china, stone- and earthenware—

Dan
Never mind that.

WORKMAN
(*Peering at him and then hurrying forward.*)
Murchison, is it?

DAN
Yes.

WORKMAN
(*Grasping his hand.*)
Welcome, brother. You're late.

DAN
The Highlanders stopped me at the bridge.

WORKMAN
They didn't search you.

DAN
But found nothing. I carry it in my head.

WORKMAN
They had no right to do that.

DAN
All suspicious persons, they said—and long live the king.

WORKMAN
But not too long, eyh?

DAN
Who's in there?

WORKMAN
The leaders—the MacDonalds, Colonel Cotton, Colonel MacLeod, the MacLeans, Campbells, MacNeills, old Kenneth Black—I've got the names of them all. Such speechmaking you never heard, and praising of each other to the skies and telling of the brave days of old—Highlanders forever, they cry out, and drinking to the bride and groom.

DAN
Ah—

WORKMAN
Them that's to be wedded tomorrow even—my master it is, Donald MacDonald.

DAN
Yours?

WORKMAN
I'm his clerk, but I don't serve him all the time—hah-hah. Have you got good news?

DAN
It is.

WORKMAN
Come on, Bob Rowan's waiting for you.

DAN
When do they break up?

WORKMAN
The Lord knows. Come on.
   (*As Dan makes no move.*)
What is it?

Dan

(*After a moment.*)
How many Liberty boys across the creek?

Workman

Some twenty or thirty. Why?

Dan

Twenty or thirty.

Workman

(*Staring at him.*)
And we're to be meek as mice with all these thousands of Highlanders gathering.

Dan

(*Muttering.*)
Yea, meek as mice.
(*Abruptly.*)
The—ah—MacDonalds and MacNeills—are they staying in your master's house?

Workman

(*Gesturing to the right front.*)
Right here—at his grandfather's, old Hugh MacDonald's. S—s—sh.
(*Taking Dan by the arm he pulls him over to the right rear and stands in the shadow. Jennie Bhan MacNeill comes into the scene from the right front, swinging a baby in her arms and crooning to it.*)

Jennie Bhan

Hush ye, my bairnie, my bonnie wee laddie,
When ye're a man ye shall follow your daddie,
Lift me a coo and a goat and a wether,
Bringing them hame to yer minnie thegither.

Dan

(*Calling presently.*)
Miss Jennie?

Jennie Bhan

(*As Dan enters through the little gate.*)
Huh? Lordy mercy, Dan Murchison—what are you doing in this place?

Dan

I want to speak with you—

Jennie Bhan

(*With sudden anger.*)
Nanh—nanh—you don't either.

Dan

I want you to give a message to—

Jennie Bhan

And I want nothing to do with you. And let me tell you that if any of that crowd in the state house find you here it'll be too bad for you. They're mad enough to kill you—you running off and joining up with old Alec MacAllister and spreading the pizen of rebellion wherever you go. Off with you or I'll call the watch.

Colonel MacAllister (*played by Allan Frank*) pleads with his Highland neighbors to join the American cause

The Cape Fear Highlanders (1940 production) honor Flora MacDonald (played by Katherine Moran) with the Highland Fling (danced by the Flora MacDonald College girls)

THE HIGHLAND CALL

Workman
(*From the rear.*)
Come on.

Dan
Then go ahead and call him. I want you to tell Miss Peggy—

Jennie Bhan
I'll tell her nothing, Dan Murchison. Get from here.

Dan
You used to have a kind word for me—

Jennie Bhan
(*Wagging her head.*)
Yeh, yeh—oh, but I'm flustered to death with all this mommicking of Whig and Tory! Leave me alone.
(*A soldier comes in at the right rear carrying a musket on his shoulder. The workman goes off quickly at the left rear.*)

Soldier
(*Saluting.*)
Pardon, mum, but is he disturbing you?

Jennie Bhan
(*Suddenly singing.*)
  Hush ye, my bairnie, my bonnie wee lammie,
  Routh o' guid things ye shall bring tae yer mammie;
  Hare frae the meadow, and deer—

DAN
It's this—tell Mistress Peggy I've got to see her—
(He turns and goes out through the gate.)

SOLDIER
Are you a Whig?

DAN
Are you a Tory?

SOLDIER
This side the creek is loyalist ground.

DAN
Yes, tonight it is.
(He goes away at the left rear.)

SOLDIER
I don't like his looks.

JENNIE BHAN
And what would a Whig be doing here at old Hugh MacDonald's house—and he smoking at the ears with his heat for the king?

SOLDIER
True, mum.
(He starts walking his post again, going back the way he came. Jennie goes on singing to the baby.)

JENNIE BHAN
Lulla-bye, lulla-bye, bonnie wee dearie,
Sleep come and close the een heavy and wearie,

Closed are the wearie een, rest ye are takin'—
Sound be your sleepin', and bright be your wakin'.

(*Anne MacLeod enters from the left rear.*)

ANNE
(*Coming through the gate and reaching her arms for the baby.*)
Come on, my precious—Has he been much trouble, Cousin Jennie?

JENNIE BHAN
Babies are always trouble. But then I was glad of an excuse not to go to that banquet. Are they finished?

ANNE
Yes.

JENNIE BHAN
And I reckon Flory made 'em a big speech.

ANNE
(*Taking the baby.*)
No, but Father did.

JENNIE BHAN
Well, I knew one of 'em would. Did anybody fight?

ANNE
(*Laughing.*)
No.

JENNIE BHAN
I'm surprised. It's hard to get two Scotchmen together without somebody fighting.

Anne

Come on, darling.

(She goes out at the right front. Jennie Bhan stands staring before her a moment, and then sinks down on the seat, her face full of thought. A medley of voices, chattering and mumbling, is heard at the back and the people begin entering at the right and left rear. They are all in holiday spirits. Some of them are carrying lanterns. In front come the MacDonalds—Allan, Flora, Donald, Old Hugh, Alexander, James, Alexander MacLeod, and Peggy MacNeill. Walking with them are Colonel Cotton and Farquhar Campbell, the latter a tall striking man of some thirty-five or forty. Behind them come a number of townspeople, young and old.)

Allan

(Who has lost some of his seriousness and diffidence in the occasion, calling out loudly.)
Thank you! Thank you one and all. And good night everybody!

A Voice

Good night.

A Young Fellow

Let's go serenade the Liberty boys.

Another Young Fellow

And run 'em in the creek.

Others

(Including young Alexander and James.)
Come on!

THE HIGHLAND CALL

ALLAN
(*Sternly, with the sudden authority of a leader.*)
We forbid that! Let this evening end peacefully.

CAMPBELL
We command you to your homes now.

ANOTHER VOICE
But we're not sleepy.

STILL ANOTHER VOICE
On to the Whigs!

COTTON
There is a martial order against breaking the peace.

ALLAN
The Whigs are on their side of the creek. Let them stay.

A VOICE
And they better stay there.

OLD HUGH
(*Calling out in his high quavery voice.*)
Good night, good night. Come, Allan, Flory, let's go in.

PEOPLE
(*Ad lib.*)
Good night, Mistress Flory. God bless you.
(*Several girls run up and kiss her hand, then kiss Peggy's hand and skip away at the left rear followed by the other townspeople, with the exception of Campbell and Cotton.*)

COTTON
(*Clicking his heels.*)
And you, sir and madam, good night. We all are deeply indebted to you. You already mark the enthusiasm of the people for your coming.

FLORA
We are grateful for their kindness.

OLD HUGH
No false modesty now, Flory. Go on in and get your sleep.
(*Young Alexander and James go out at the right front.*)

CAMPBELL
You are the Highlander heroine, and you, sir, their chief.

OLD HUGH
And only say the word, Allan, and we'll obey.

ALLAN
A grave responsibility you've put upon us.

FLORA
And may we measure up to it.
(*Extending her hand.*)
Good night, sir.
(*Campbell and Cotton kiss her hand in turn.*)

CAMPBELL
And good night to you, Donald and Peggy. A happy life for you both.

THE HIGHLAND CALL

Donald
Thank you.

Allan
You'll spend the night with us, Cousin Jennie?

Jennie Bhan
No, I'm staying over at Hector's house. I'll go in and kiss the baby good night.

Old Hugh
(*As she starts off.*)
Looks like you'd be tired of babies, Jennie.
(*To the air.*)
She's only had nine of her own.

Jennie Bhan
Huh, I wish I could start all over again with nine more. Tonight I do.
(*She sticks her finger in Old Hugh's tummy and goes out.*)

Old Hugh
(*Cackling.*)
She's a case.

Cotton
Is she Whig or Tory?

Old Hugh
Canny Jennie Bhan! If there's trouble, she's likely to put half her boys on one side and half on the other to be safe. Off to bed, everybody.
(*He goes in.*)

Campbell
(*Bowing.*)
And now until tomorrow.

Others
Till tomorrow.

Cotton
And I doubt not before the day is done we can have a roster of three thousand able-bodied men.

Campbell
That will be enough.

Cotton
Enough to insure the peace.
  (*He salutes and with Campbell turns and goes out at the left rear.*)

Donald
Let's walk down to Cool Spring a moment, Peggy, the hall was so stuffy—you need the fresh air.

Peggy
I'm tired, Donald, perhaps—no, not tonight. Thank you.

Donald
There are some plans for the reception tomorrow evening—

Peggy
I'm—I'm tired—good night, good night, everybody.
  (*She turns hurriedly and goes away at the right. Donald stands looking after her.*)

Allan
(*To Flora.*)
Did you hear what they said—three thousand men?

Flora
I heard.
(*Fervently.*)
And that will mean order will be kept. It will.

Donald
(*Who has continued to stare in the direction Peggy has gone.*)
What's the matter with Peggy?

Flora
(*Consolingly.*)
She's only tired—it was a hard trip here.

Donald
(*Shaking his head.*)
There's something on her mind, has been for several days.

Flora
After tomorrow it will all be settled.

Donald
I don't understand her.
(*Now shaking his shoulders as if to throw off his worrying thought.*)
Good night.

Allan and Flora
Good night.

ALLAN
And good luck in the tournament tomorrow.

DONALD
Thank you.
(*He goes away at the right rear.*)

ALLAN
What think you, Flory?

FLORA
That Peggy and Donald will not be married a minute too soon.

ALLAN
Yes, that too. But the reception, Flory—
(*With sudden jubilancy.*)
Ah, how wonderful it is to see so many of our old friends again.

FLORA
But it is more wonderful to live quietly at Killiegrey, Allan.

ALLAN
Yea.

FLORA
And we must hurry back there—soon, Allan, soon.

ALLAN
Day after tomorrow we will—if all goes well.

Flora
And it will go well. Our people are united—there will be no trouble.
> (*He puts his arm around her and they go away at the right front. The scene is deserted for an instant. The soldier enters at the rear slowly pacing his beat in front of the state house. The chorus begins softly humming "The Highland Widow's Lament," and he stops as if listening to it. Peggy comes out and sits on the little bench at the right front. And now the soldier begins humming with the chorus. Finally Peggy joins in, and the scene gradually becomes imbued with the low drowsy lament. After a moment, Jennie Bhan comes hurriedly in at the right and the music obediently dies.*)

Jennie Bhan
> (*Looking up at the sky, as she stops in front of Peggy.*)

Not a cloud—the moon as bright as a shoebuckle. The weather will be fine tomorrow. That's a good sign, Peggy.
> (*As if quoting.*)

Blest be the bride the sun shines on.
> (*She sits down.*)

Peggy
You said you wanted to talk with me.

Jennie Bhan
Oh, nothing in particular.
> (*Twisting in her seat.*)

Mind if I suck my pipe?

PEGGY

Of course not.

JENNIE BHAN

It's a life-saver sometimes.
(*She lights her pipe and is silent a moment, then clears her throat.*)
You certainly are no joy to look at, Peggy MacNeill.

PEGGY

I've got a headache, maybe that's the reason. And I haven't slept much lately.

JENNIE BHAN

Oooh, that's too bad. Must have something on your mind. What do you think about?

PEGGY

Oh—everything—the woods at Killiegrey, the spring, the autumn colors, the sunset—all that we've left there!
(*She bows her head over in her hands.*)

JENNIE BHAN

(*Half-angrily.*)
Danged if I understand you young folks any more. They ain't like what I used to be. Why, the night before I married my scrubblin Archibald I slept dead to the world. Didn't even dream about him. And when I marched up before the parson my heart was light as a bird. I was happy. You're not happy. What's the matter with you?

PEGGY

Nothing.

THE HIGHLAND CALL

JENNIE BHAN

Here all ready to marry the finest man in the Cape Fear River Valley, and you look like somebody had up and died on you.

(*Peggy is silent.*)

Go ahead and tell me about it.

PEGGY

There's nothing to tell—nothing.

JENNIE BHAN

Look at me, Peggy MacNeill. If you don't love Donald who do you love?

PEGGY

I still love him—in a way I do—

JENNIE BHAN

Then it's doing you the least good of anybody I ever saw.

PEGGY

Maybe not the way I used to. Oh, it's the truth, Cousin Jennie.

JENNIE BHAN

Who else is there?

(*Throwing up her hands as Peggy is silent.*)

Ah, you're crazy in the head, and Lord help Donald with a lunatic wife.

PEGGY

I am not.

Jennie Bhan

Ah, it's from walking bareheaded under the moon. There's an old saying about that—
 (*Spitting.*)
And ain't I got in my cedar chest letters from you in Scotland all about Donald. Donald this and Donald that, and everything was Donald. And what a breaking of your heart it was when he came away to the new world.

Peggy

But that was Scotland.

Jennie Bhan

Love is love, wherever it is—
 (*Snorting.*)
And he loves you better than life itself. That's enough. As soon as you're married to him everything will be all right. Evening brings the cattle home. Let me tell you a secret. Your Aunt Flora didn't love your Uncle Allan before she married him. Now he's the apple of her eye.

Peggy

Anybody could love Uncle Allan—he's so kind and good and—

Jennie Bhan

And Donald's kind and good too. Course he likes the almighty shilling, and sometimes that's not so bad.

Peggy

Who did Aunt Flory love—Prince Charlie?—I've heard it whispered so. Foolish too.

JENNIE BHAN

It don't make no difference who it was—prince or pauper—She loves Allan now, and has made him a good wife and mother—no better in the world. Now you go back to bed and day after tomorrow morning when you wake up the world will be a different place, and from then on the sun will rise and set in Donald. Why, my goodness, ain't he one of the handsomest fellows about? And ain't he wealthy? And a leader here in town? And going to be one of the greatest men in this colony? And you've got no reason to back and hedge about him. But why do you say, "Foolish too?"

(*Angrily, as Peggy remains silent.*)

If you was my child, you know what I'd do?

PEGGY

Please, Cousin Jennie.

JENNIE BHAN

I'd go back in the pantry and get down the strop and—Oh, I'm hardhearted, I know it.

(*Blowing her nose with a great checkered handkerchief.*)

And it ain't like me. So I just as well break down and tell you. I can still see that fellow's eyes like two big pitiful moons a-pleading at me.—Young Dan Murchison's here in town!

PEGGY

Dan!

JENNIE BHAN

"Dan" she says, same as Ben Franklin's 'lectricity had hit her.

PEGGY

He's in danger here.

JENNIE BHAN

He's not maybe, but everybody else is. Well, I've told you like I knowed I would. It's my soft heart. But heart is just as important as head. Take your choice.

PEGGY
(*Flinging her arms around Jennie Bhan.*)
You're good—good.

JENNIE BHAN

I'm not advising you, understand, not telling you what to do.
(*As a croaking song is heard at the rear.*)
Bah, look at that fool.
(*Old Sandy Ochiltree comes in drunk. He is supported by Simey, who still wears his Indian garb but minus bow and arrows.*)

SANDY
(*Singing.*)
  O, Gilderoy was a bonnie boy;
  Had roses till his shoon;
  His stockings were of silken soy,
  Wi' garters hanging doun.
  It was, I ween—
I'm Sandy Ochiltree, Lord of the Western Isles—hic—being brought home from the club by my servant—
(*Slapping Simey around the shoulders affectionately.*)

JENNIE BHAN MACNEILL (*played by Josephine Sharkey*) gives PEGGY MACNEILL (*played by Helen Bailey*) some advice in her troubled love affair

WOOTTEN-MOULTON

THE HIGHLAND CALL CHORUS, of Fayetteville, North Carolina, directed by Virginia Harlin

Servant, Simey, and by the paps of Jura, I love you—
Club, did I say?—a little stewed, pickled some or otherwise, but in good shape notwithstanding—
(*Singing.*)
>He was my joy and heart's delight,
>My handsome Gilderoy.

(*Bowing low.*)
Even, dames, good evening, ladies all. And is that you, Cousin Jennie, the fair one?

JENNIE BHAN
It's me and get on away from here with your caterwauling.

SANDY
Spit out your pipe and give us a kiss.
(*While he is talking Dan Murchison comes in at the left front, suddenly stops and then withdraws into the shadow.*)

JENNIE BHAN
I'll kiss you in the face with my fist if you mess with me.
(*To Simey.*)
Take him on back there, and put him to bed in the barn—no, in the stable. Stable, understand?

SIMEY
Oohm.

SANDY
Lord, what a celebration we've had. All the music and the clapping and the cheering and every time they'd drink a toast there in the big hall—hic—I'd crook both me arms

and let her go down—ahm—in the cellar there. And my bodyguard here standing by to take me home. Eigh, Simey boy?

SIMEY
Oohm—

SANDY
Hah—hah—hear him say he loves me.
  (*Singing.*)
> He was a braw gallant
> And he played at the glove
> And the bonnie Earl of Murray
> Oh, he was the queen's love.

JENNIE BHAN
(*Rising and beginning to push him off at the right.*)
Out with you.

SANDY
And it's a war we're going to have. Did you hear me, a war?

JENNIE BHAN
Scat!

SANDY
And I'm all set to be a soldier here with my armor-bearer, my gun-toter. Ha-ha. And that old Killiegrey place and the wild woods with the varmints, no more for me, no more for me. In the thick and the thin of the smoke and the cutting you'll find me.
  (*Bringing his arm down through the air with a swish.*)

THE HIGHLAND CALL

Whoosh, by Arthur's oven, and off comes another Whig's head—
(*Looking down at the empty ground.*)
—And whose head will I cut off first? That Dan Murchison—for the great persecution and tribulation he put upon me.
(*Calling into the night.*)
Beware of Sandy Ochiltree's thirsty blade—hah-hah! And I'll be making—
(*Lowering his voice.*)
—a pretty piece of money from it too. There's a price on his head. There in the court house Colonel Cotton and them others are making out a list. I just heard 'em. And he's at the top, get him first they say. Get Dan Murchison first.

Jennie Bhan

And you, get out. Get out!
(*Taking his arm.*)
Come on, I'll see you put up.
(*She and Simey lead him away into the darkness. She calls back.*)
Go on in the house, Peggy. Good night, and I've had my say.

Peggy

Good night.
(*She rises and turns away to the right when Dan steps swiftly into the scene.*)

Dan

Peggy.

Peggy
(Whirling about.)
Oh—
(He comes over towards her.)
You must get away from here. Sandy says there's—
(She takes an impulsive step to him and then suddenly stops.)

Dan
I heard him, and thank him for the warning.

Peggy
It's dangerous for you. It is.

Dan
But not enough to keep me from seeing you. Ah, Peggy, you've got to listen to me.

Peggy
No, Dan, you are our enemy now.

Dan
Not yours, but your people's. They are wrong, wrong, and Colonel MacAllister and Lillington and Harnett and the Whig leaders are right. The Highlanders are blind and don't see what's happening in this country. In their pride and selfishness they think they can stop this movement that's started. But they can't. Things are breaking up, changing from one end of the country to the other. The old order is bound to pass away, and a new one is coming.

Peggy

There's no power here strong enough to win against the king, Dan. Aunt Flora's right.

Dan

And in the new day—all these differences will be wiped out. Just like I said—there won't be any high and low—some sitting up near the throne of God, and some the dregs of the earth. We'll all be free and equal before the law, and there'll be a chance for every man to prove himself.
  (*Vehemently.*)
And I'll prove myself, for you I will, Peggy.

Peggy

It won't be like that, Dan. It'll never be like that.

Dan

It will. Everywhere the common people are coming together, and it's not for hate of somebody else or money or place, the way it's been in the old world—but for a dream they've got, this dream of freedom and self-government—men walking the earth like kings in their own right, servants to nobody but themselves. I tell you nothing can stop us.

Peggy
  (*Her voice suddenly changing.*)
If it could be like that, ever like that! Sometimes for a second I seem to see how it could be. And then I know I'm wrong, and Aunt Flora and Uncle Allan and Donald and the rest of them are right.

DAN

(*Hotly.*)
Then the power of our arms will prove they're wrong, the way they've started on the battlefields of the north—at Bunker Hill and Lexington.

PEGGY

(*Gazing at him.*)
In the night I lie awake thinking and sometimes it shines before me like a light and I feel that Cousin Alec is right. And we are wrong, and there will be a war and our side will be destroyed and this dream you talk about will come true, and then—this thing that holds me—grips me—will be broken—

DAN

It will!

PEGGY

And then in the morning, in the brightness of day, all that I've been thinking seems foolish and like a dream. And the strength of my people, all their history and glory and what they've meant and what I mean to them—grips me closer than before.
(*Shaking her head.*)
You don't know what it means, this call—this kinship. Back in Scotland they knew what it was, they still know what it is. It's something that holds these Highlanders together stronger than life, stronger than death. In its name they commit murder, kill—

DAN

But it's not stronger than love. And I love you, Peggy MacNeill, I always have. You've been my star, high above

me and yet tonight you're close enough. I love you, I tell you. And nothing will ever take you from me.
(*Fiercely.*)
Nothing.

Peggy

(*Shuddering.*)
No. They are too powerful for you. Uncle Allan and Donald and Colonel Cotton and the governor and the king, all against you. They'll kill you.
(*Half-sobbing.*)
You are fine and great and they will kill you.
(*Her eyes bright and feverish.*)
And in this prison house that closes me around, I tell you now—through the bars of it I see the sunlight, and there's joy and the wonder of things there, and it's all you, Dan—

Dan

(*His voice tremulous with joy.*)
Peggy.

Peggy

And through the bars I reach my hand to touch yours but it will never be more than that. Tomorrow I will marry him.

Dan

(*Dropping her hand which he has seized.*)
Then I am not any glory and wonder to you, nothing but a down-and-out poor servant, and you are still the great MacNeill of Barra. And I—I'm hungry and homeless— I wander the earth from one place to another getting a crust here, a bed in somebody's haystack there. I have nothing to offer you but my love, but someday there'll be

a place for you—we will build it together then. That's the future I see ahead. I've come to beg you—

Peggy

And I'd follow you ragged and homeless if I could. But he has my plighted word.
   (*Fiercely.*)
Do you know what that means? There in Scotland before he left we stood before the altar, our hands upon the sacred book, and swore a solemn oath to be true to each other till death. And it was signed and written down.
   (*Half sobbing.*)
I knew it all the time. I knew I was bound—and yet there in Killiegrey I began to forget it—lost in a dream—happy there. With my mind I knew it couldn't be like that, and yet I hoped something would happen, maybe half expected something to happen and I could go on staying there and—and—I would be free—But nothing happened.

Dan

Then something shall.
   (*Wildly.*)
I'll break that oath for you. Somehow I will.

Peggy

And good-by—good—
   (*She turns away and then springs back and flings her arms around his neck.*)
It's you I love—you forever—Dan—
   (*She clings to him. Flora comes into the scene from the right.*)

THE HIGHLAND CALL

FLORA
(In a low voice.)
Peggy.

PEGGY
Yes.
(Turning away from Dan.)
—I know—all about pride and family, Aunt Flora—go ahead and say it.

FLORA
(Sadly.)
Ah, more than that. Peggy—Yea for both of us in the days ahead. Come.
(They go away at the right. For a moment Dan stands with his head bent, then his fists relax and, turning, he hurries away at the left rear. Old Sandy comes wobbling in at the right rear. Simey is following him.)

SANDY
So you put me in the stable, hah?—
(Brushing the tail of his kilt.)
—there with the cows, and you messing up my gay garment, and what would I be wearing tomorrow at the wedding.
(He comes over by the bench.)
Ahm—I'll guard the house.
(As he sinks down Simey runs around and sits down with his feet extended. Sandy lays his head blissfully in his lap.)

SIMEY
Oohm—oohm—

Sandy

(*Chuckling.*)

Hah, hah. I was going to beat you tomorrow but I won't. Oooh, my head is one big coal of red-hot fire—fan me.

(*He goes to sleep. The watchman comes wandering across the scene at the rear tinkling his bell.*)

Watchman

(*In a sleepy call.*)

Half by the clock and all is well in the town—all is well! God save his majesty the king!

(*He drifts out at the right. The light dies from the stage and comes up on Mr. Mac.*)

Mr. Mac

And so they waited for tomorrow, and up and down the length of the Cape Fear Valley, on highway and byroad, in hamlet and home, east of the river and west of the river, and around this very spot where we are gathered tonight the strange turmoil of events and things was at work—at work to what fulfillment we shall see. As the poet has said—

> Much as the seasons come and go, as the days to their appointed end,
> So do the making and breaking of nations come to pass,
> The building up and breaking down,
> The collision, the overruling, the riding on to victory,
> The retiring and the flight of defeat.
> As time continueth on her swift foot, so doth an idea walking abroad in the world.
> Can kings or counselors hinder it? Can a weakling bring it to pass?

And slowly, ever so slowly through the years, these lines of division had become clearer—on the one hand a strong and centralized government—a government to which men owed undying and absolute obedience and which exercised its right over them through the authority of a divine right grounded in a ritual out of heaven; on the other a democratic government which exercised only these rights freely given to it by the consent of the governed. One was of God, they said, the other of man, one of obedience and law, the other of liberty and free will. Mysterious and strange these principles of human nature. And even today they continue to clash with each other in the world —the question whether the state is supreme or whether the individual is. And it is not to be wondered at that the Highlanders, who for generations had served their chieftains, and now more lately one great chieftain the king, should swear their continued devotion to the cause they believed to be as solid and right as the earth on which they walked. But there were men in the colonies who believed otherwise—such as Sam Adams in Boston, James Madison, Thomas Jefferson, and more lately George Washington himself. There are, they said, certain rights and liberties belonging to men prior to all other considerations—rights irrespective of nationality, race, creed, color or previous condition of servitude or class. These belong to men as men, and are born when they are born—the rights of life, liberty, and the pursuit of happiness. And only a government based upon a recognition of these principles can function freely and survive.

Thus the two views opposed each other, views as strong and deep as life itself, and the hour had come as many feared and too many knew, when the battlefield must decide the issue. And in the head-on collision between these two doctrines of government, as always happens, the price must be paid with tragedy and pain. So it was that in the lives of Dan Murchison and Peggy MacNeill and Flora MacDonald and her family, all the strains and hurt of the woeful times were symbolized. The very birth-pangs of the republic were theirs. There were thousands of others like them—up and down the land, along this valley, caught in the tension and breaking of old loyalties and new hopes, the clash of duty with love, of friendship against friendship, family against family, brother against brother, and father against son.

(The light fades out from Mr. Mac and comes up on the center stage as the organ begins to play "God Save the King.")

SCENE 2

The scene is one of dazzling brightness in the evening sun, and made more brilliant by the striking costumes of the Highlanders gathered along the stage near the state house and spilling off down the street on either side. Everyone is dressed in holiday attire, and the different plaids of the many clans make an attractive and intriguing picture. On a sort of platform at the back are Flora MacDonald, Allan, Peggy, Donald, Old Hugh MacDonald, and other members of the household. At the right rear at a little table are a clerk and Colonel Cotton. Farquhar Campbell is in the center rear of the scene. At the right and left are a few soldiers and two flag bearers. When the curtain rises, all the people are singing loudly and joyfully "God Save the King," accompanied by the chorus and the organ.

PEOPLE

God save our Lord the King,
Long live our noble King,
  God save the King.
Send him victorious,
Happy and glorious,
Long to reign over us,
  God save the King.

O, Lord, our God arise,
Scatter his enemies,
  And make them fall,

Confound their politics,
Frustrate their knavish tricks
On thee our hopes we fix.
    God save us all.

(*Donald MacDonald lifts his bonnet and waves it in the air.*)

DONALD
(*Leading the cheer.*)
Long live the king!

PEOPLE
(*With a great roar.*)
Long live the king! the king! the king!
(*Now the flag bearers straighten the flags up and stand at attention.*)

CAMPBELL
(*Looking about him and calling loudly.*)
Is there anybody else? Anybody else?
(*A young nondescript fellow some twenty years old pushes through the crowd at the left. Pulling off his cap and revealing his head covered with a kind of skull cap made of a red handkerchief, he bows low to Allan and Flora MacDonald.*)

YOUNG MAN
Greetings, sir, and my lady.

ALLAN
Greetings to you.

THE HIGHLAND CALL

Young Man
(*Laconically as he looks around at the gathering.*)
I want to sign that there book. Up the road they were telling how you were rounding up everybody.

Allan
Your name?

Young Man
Fanning, Dave Fanning. I'm not a Highlander but I'll sign.

Campbell
(*To Colonel Cotton.*)
Dave Fanning, Colonel.
(*He gestures and Fanning goes over to the table.*)

Fanning
If there's any Whigs anybody wants killed just give me their names. I'm r'aring to ride and fight for the king.

Allan
(*Sternly.*)
We're not enlisting soldiers here today.

Fanning
Then what you doing, your honor?

Allan
It's a holiday.

Campbell
A Highlander get-together.
(*Genially.*)
And we've done that, haven't we, folks?

People
We have that. Yes, sir. You're right.

Fanning
Put my name down in that there book. Dave Fanning from the crotch of Deep River and the Haw.

Cotton
Sign there.

Fanning
I can't write—not yet.

Cotton
Your mark.
(Fanning makes his mark. Campbell speaks to Colonel Cotton and then turns and addresses the assembly triumphantly.)

Campbell
This has been a great day for us all, and joyous it is to see you gathered here, happy and united in heart and mind. And now we will hear the names of the clans represented here today.

Voices
Yes, read 'em. Let's hear 'em.
(At a gesture from Colonel Cotton the clerk stands up and begins to read from the book in a rolling spout of words.)

Clerk
Buchanan, Cameron, Campbell, Clark, Ferguson, Forbes, Frazier, Gordon, Graham, Lamont, Logan, MacAuley,

MacCormick, MacDonald, MacDougald, McInnis, McIntyre, MacKay, McKeithan, McLaren, MacLaughlin, McLean, MacLeod, MacMillan, MacNeill, McPherson, MacRae, MacRainey, Monroe, Murray, Ross, Shaw, Sinclair, Stewart, Sutherland.
(He sits down suddenly and there is a round of applause.)

CAMPBELL
A roster of—
(Impressively.)
—some three thousand names.

A VOICE
Where's the Clan MacAllister?

JENNIE BHAN
(Who stands over at the left surrounded by several stalwart young Scotchmen.)
Yea, where is he? You will not find MacAllister here. Old Alec's got himself all herded off somewhere breeding mischief.
(A murmur rises among the people. Sandy, who has been standing over at the right, in a nervous flurry moves towards Colonel Cotton, still carrying his old bagpipe strung across his shoulder. Simey, wearing an Indian headdress, follows behind him.)

SANDY
(Bowing low.)
Please, your excellence, I didn't hear you read out the Clan Ochiltree.
(There is a burst of laughter from the people. Sandy looks around and nods in good humor.)

Oh, you may laugh, but it was a name to spread terror once to the heart of man, it was. There in the hills of Scotland —and all pedigreed back to Adam's day.

CAMPBELL

(*To the clerk.*)
One of Laird MacDonald's men, already numbered.

SANDY

True, I'm his man, and valiant till death. But please, sir, put it down in its own right and privilege—and with one brother and bodyguard attached.
(*Indicating Simey.*)
They do say that to be in a book is to 'mortalize....

COTTON

Write.
(*The clerk writes.*)

CLERK

Clan Ochiltree, represented by—

SANDY

(*Bowing again.*)
—By us—Sandy and Simey—Darach MacDarach, sons of Og, son of Og—Ochiltree. You got it, sir?

COTTON

It's down.

CAMPBELL

(*Calling.*)
Anybody else? Any-body—else?

(*No one answers.*)
And now, fellow Scotsmen—
(*Suddenly clapping his hands.*)
Music, music!
(*The organ strikes up a gay sprightly dance, and several young girls dressed in gay fetching costumes dance in from the right and left and do the Highland Fling. The people gradually get infected by the movements and the music. Some of them begin to clap their hands. And now the chorus starts to hum a thumping accompaniment with the organ. Old Sandy takes his bagpipe from around his shoulders and plays gleefully away, now and then cutting a few steps along with the dancers. Simey mimics him, the palm of his hand going in front of his lips like an Indian making his call. Jennie Bhan begins to cut a few steps and so do some of the young people around the fringe of the crowd. Finally the dance winds up as the girls prance out the way they came. Cheers, whistles, and calls go after them. Sandy and Simey start to follow, then turn shamefacedly back as one of the crowd shouts at them. The organ gradually dies down.*)

ALLAN
(*Leaning towards Flora, his face beaming.*)
Wonderful.
(*He applauds again.*)

CAMPBELL
And now—
(*At this moment a messenger runs in from the right. He hurries up to Campbell and tips his hat.*)
What is it?

Messenger
For the Reverend MacLeod, sir.

Campbell
(*Nodding towards MacLeod who is standing at the rear near Donald.*)
You sir, Mr. MacLeod.
(*MacLeod steps down.*)

MacLeod
(*To the messenger.*)
What is it?

Messenger
You are needed down at the bridge at once, sir.

Donald
(*Calling out.*)
Do you know this fellow?

MacLeod
No.

Messenger
Yea, but you do, sir. My mother goes to hear you preach every Sunday at Barbecue Church. Poor Betty Cutts, you know her, sir.

MacLeod
I do.

Cotton
(*Standing up.*)
Who is this fellow?

MacLeod
It's quite all right, Colonel. I know his mother, a God-fearing woman. I will tend to her and return immediately.

Messenger
Thank you, thank you. And she will pass away happy.

Donald
But if so ill what is she doing here, twenty miles from home?

Messenger
Please you, sir, she came to see the fun and frolic and joy in the great splurge of the people. But the Lord struck her down, and she lies breathing out her last gasp to the world there by the bridge head. She wants to see her preacher, sir.

MacLeod
Come.

Messenger
And you too, sir, Master Donald MacDonald. If you would but come give her a final word she would bless you from here to heaven, sir.

Cotton
By gad, we'll all go.

Donald
I don't know the woman.

Messenger
You do, sir. But remember. She held you at your christening in the old world, she did.

Donald

(*Muttering.*)
Nay, perhaps.
(*With sudden sharpness to Colonel Cotton.*)
Colonel Cotton, send a guard with the Reverend MacLeod.

Cotton

Good. In these times we must be careful. Two men with you, Corporal.
(*He gestures and three of the Highland soldiers come over and stand by the preacher.*)

MacLeod

I have no need of these. We are all friends here.

Cotton

Not at the bridge—the Whigs begin there. Be watchful.

Jennie Bhan

Sure, and we need the preacher for the wedding.

Campbell

Indeed we do. You're the only one in fifty miles to perform the ceremony.

MacLeod

There is no danger. I'll return immediately.
(*The soldiers salute and follow MacLeod out.*)

Messenger

(*Obsequiously, to those about him.*)
Thank you, thank you, kind people. Thank you one and all.

THE HIGHLAND CALL

(*He pulls his cap hurriedly on and dives off at the right.*)

CAMPBELL

(*Giving his arm a sweep around the scene.*)
And now, ladies and gentlemen, I give you the soon to be —bride and groom—
(*Donald and Peggy stand up and the people cheer them. In the meantime a few servants have been going around among the crowd serving cups of drinks, and now the cups are lifted aloft and Campbell leads in a toast.*)
To Donald MacDonald and Peggy MacNeill!

VOICES

MacDonald! MacNeill! Hurrah, hurrah! A long life—forever!
(*The organ strikes up again in a gay tune, and now the girls come dancing in from the right and left doing a Highland reel to the tune of "Polwart on the Green." As before, the people enter into the spirit of the dance and the chorus likewise. At the second and third turn of the figure the people begin to clap their hands and sing "tra-la-la" in accompaniment. And the chorus adds a shrill, joyous whistling of the melody. The dance grows more abandoned, and soon most of the people on the stage are swirling about in a semi-circle behind the dancers. Donald pulls Peggy out and they join the mad scramble. The older people keep their positions on the platform at the back and look on with amusement and good cheer. Presently the crowd separates and gathers on the right and left, leaving a space immediately in front of Flora and*)

Allan open. Now the dancing girls turn their backs to the audience in the theater and perform especially for Flora and her husband. Flora nods and smiles and for the moment forgets whatever fear and care are haunting her. The girls finish their dance with a low curtsy, and Flora stands up as they crowd eagerly forward and kiss her hand. Campbell, the easeful master of ceremonies, goes on with another announcement.)

CAMPBELL

And now, ladies and gentlemen, friends, loyal Gaels all, a word from the man who has made this day possible! He will bring us greetings from his excellency, Governor Martin, who unfortunately is ill aboard his cruiser at Wilmington. Colonel Cotton!

(*The people applaud and Cotton arises with military stiffness.*)

COTTON

I am not a speaker but a military man. In place of words I believe in deeds. Suffice it to say that his excellency the governor sends his greetings and regrets. Only an act of God could keep him away today. He thanks you one and all for your continued devotion and loyalty in the past and counts upon the same for the future. And it will be a source of great satisfaction when I convey to him this book with the names of so many of his people written there.

(*He sits down. The people applaud.*)

CAMPBELL

You—Cousin Jennie.

A Voice
(*Calling out.*)
Speech!—Speech, Jennie Bhan.
   (*Another voice takes up the cry.*)

Jennie Bhan
(*Loudly.*)
Now, you folks behave yourselves. You know I ain't going to make no speech.

Campbell
Come on, Cousin Jennie. Give the people a few words of greeting.

Jennie Bhan
Howdy.
   (*Suddenly some of the girls close to her begin running around her, holding hands and chanting.*)

Girls
Jennie Bhan, Jennie Bhan, Jennie Bhan the weaver,
Thousand sheep and cattle pens, the richest on the river.
Jennie Bhan, Jennie Bhan, Jennie Bhan the weaver,
Mother of the Highland clans, we canna bear to leave her.
   (*Jennie Bhan breaks through the circle and stands out in the middle of the scene fanning herself in a pleased vexatious flurry.*)

Voices
Speech! Speech!

Jennie Bhan

Now why you want me to talk any, I don't know. I got a tongue long as from here to Hector's Bluff and back, and ain't no telling what I'll say if I get started.

A Voice

How about the time you danced with Ben Franklin?

Jennie Bhan

Oh, but there was a buck of a lad. Rambunctious he was!

A Voice

The old traitor!

Another Voice

Aye.

Another Voice

Did he dance the Highland Fling?

Jennie Bhan

No. I did.

Another Voice

Ah, that was a bird. I bet you cut up.

Jennie Bhan

I cut up some. Later Ben told me—well—you know how he talks—all that stuff he puts in his almanac. Later he said—Jennie Bhan, you certainly flung 'em a fling.
   (*The people laugh.*)
And that's as much speech as I got to say, except the fact

that I ain't never had so much fun as here today. And, Donald, I'll say this, you're the best rider I ever saw. You're better'n my John and Malcolm here. I want you to come up some time and help me herd in my cattle.

Donald
(*In high good humor.*)
I'll come and do that, Cousin Jennie.

Old Hugh
(*In his quavery voice.*)
Tell Archibald we missed him, and to hurry up and get well of them risings. He won't even be here tonight for the wedding?

Jennie Bhan
No, he won't. Well, that's about all folks. I ain't never seen such a gathering of Scotsmen in all my life as has been in this town today. I don't think any of us ever need feel lonesome wherever we are. All we got to do is to remember the thousands of our folks scattered up and down this valley. Yes, sir, there's mergens of 'em, mergens. And I reckon every one of you will remember to his dying day the fun we've had at this festival, with all the bagpipes blowing and the flags flying there on the muster ground. And Allan MacDonald there, looking like the Lord in his own chariot a-passing by.

Voices
Master Allan MacDonald! MacDonald!
(*Allan smiles good-naturedly about.*)

Jennie Bhan

I know some of you have druv over a hundred miles here to see the Highland Queen.

(*A sudden hush comes over the assembly.*)

Well, Flory, ain't no need for me to praise you. Farquhar Campbell, you do it. She needs words from a gifted tongue like yours.

Campbell

(*As Jennie shakes her head and retires.*)

We have been blessed with words of greeting and good fellowship from our chieftain, and I have prepared a speech to introduce our lady to you. But there is no need of that—

(*Loudly.*)

Flora MacDonald! The preserver of Bonnie Prince Charlie, loyal daughter of the empire and ward of his majesty, King George the Third—

(*He bows. The people are silent for an instant and then break into loud and wild applause. Flora remains seated where she is and her hand goes out and rests on Allan's arm. Finally she gazes out and then the worried, harried look comes back to her face for an instant.*)

Flora

Thank you, my dear friends, my own people.

(*Her lips trembling.*)

At this moment, I don't know what to say. I have no words for the feeling that is in me. All day has been like a dream, a beautiful dream with the sunlight over us and laughter and music and singing. As it should be here in this new world. And oh, if it could only continue like that, if all the days could be happy and full of joy ahead.

THE HIGHLAND CALL

(*Shaking her head, her voice filled with sadness.*)
And now with what I say maybe some of the brightness of this occasion will be ended. But I must say it.
(*Her voice now growing stronger with determination as she rises.*)
It hurts to speak this hard and cruel truth, but the truth must be faced however hard it is, and that truth is the horror and certainty of war.
(*A murmur rises among the people. She is silent a moment and then goes on.*)
And I had thought we were done with that, done with all these killings and the waste and tragedy there in Scotland. Month after month, day after day I've shut my eyes to this shadow darkening this new land, my ears to the sound of distant turmoil. Again and again I have said these things would pass, they were but small quarrels among misguided groups of people. But now today I know that I was wrong. And some of you know it. And all the fun and frolic of this occasion cannot drive away the fear and the apprehension that hang over us. And the gathering of the Highlanders here today has more to do with war than pleasure.
(*Colonel Cotton looks around.*)
I am sure Colonel Cotton will forgive me for speaking what we all must know within the next few days.

A Voice

(*Softly.*)
Ah, she is right.

Another Voice

It's certain to be, God help us all.

Flora

Night and day I've thought about it. All last night my husband and I talked about it, and there's no escaping it. In this country there has arisen a doctrine of liberty and anarchy, the claims of rebellious men to take authority into their own hands as they see fit. They have no such right and can never have and they must be put down. In the glory of our empire, an empire as just as it is powerful, has been my refuge and the refuge of my people.

Voices

That's right. Right. She knows.

Flora

No doubt mistakes have occurred—but gradually they would be righted if—if—I know as I am standing here today that the future peace of the world depends upon our empire. This is not a boast. It has nothing to do with pride and pomp, or wealth or power, but the union of nations under one king and common rule. Already this vast empire has begun to spread itself in the world. Far ahead, generations ahead, I can see the age when peace and good will shall reign the world over because of it. And that ideal has given me and my husband strength, has given you strength to come into this wilderness and do your part in the creation of that dream.

Voices

Hear, hear!

Flora

Would God it could be done peacefully, but it cannot. But it must be done. And we must see to it that this Cape Fear

River Valley, this great stretch of land from the ocean to the mountains, is kept in the control of Britain's loyal sons. United in a common cause we can keep the north divided from the south. That we must do. And as we keep them divided, the king's armies, with the help of loyalists everywhere, will soon be able to put down this treason.
(*She is silent and so are the people.*)
And that means we must fight. Colonel Cotton knows it Farquhar Campbell knows it. That's the reason for all the names in our roster. The names written there are the names of soldiers soon to be. And well it is so.
(*Again the people murmur and Sandy Ochiltree calls out bravely enough.*)

Sandy
That suits me. I'm ready to fight.

Voices
Me too.

Other Voices
(*More lively.*)
A war. Let it come, we'll fight. We'll show the traitors.

Flora
I have a husband and two sons here and another son who has already fought at Bunker Hill and lies wounded—
(*Abruptly, as she almost breaks down.*)

—Colonel Cotton, you can tell them.
(*She resumes her seat.*)

Colonel Cotton

(*Rising.*)
His excellency, Josiah Martin, Governor of North Carolina, has this day issued an order—
(*He pulls a document from his coat.*)
—that each and every able-bodied man shall be ready at a minute's notice and shall equip himself whenever possible with musket, powder and ball. Tomorrow you will all return to your homes and await the summons to muster. And now it gives me great pleasure to inform you that when the emergency comes you shall march under the leadership of your chieftain here, General Allan MacDonald and his aide, Captain Donald MacDonald. The Governor has so commissioned them.
(*For a moment the people are silent and then applaud. Colonel Cotton bows slightly to Flora.*)
I do not share my lady's horror of war. That is my profession and in this case I fear it not at all, for we shall win and win quickly. I am betraying no secrets when I inform you that already his majesty's government has dispatched Sir Henry Clinton from the Chesapeake with a fleet of ships and soldiers, and Sir Peter Parker will, within a few weeks, arrive from Ireland with another fleet to join us here on the Cape Fear. And with their aid and the devotion of you all we shall keep this Cape Fear Valley safe for the king!

Voices

We shall, we will. Long live the king! And Colonel Cotton!

COLONEL MACALLISTER (*played by Allan Frank*) pleads with FLORA MACDONALD (*played by Katherine Moran*) to join the American cause and thereby save herself from banishment

Captain Dan Murchison (*played by Douglass Watson*, 1939 production) brings news of the Declaration of Independence

THE HIGHLAND CALL

OTHER VOICES

'Ray for Colonel Cotton.

(*At this moment the organ begins an ominous and monotonous drum in the pedals from the tune "The Bonny Earl of Murray." As it continues, the people look about them uncertainly and then draw back to the rear. Colonel Alexander MacAllister enters at the right front accompanied by some six or eight young Whigs dressed in buckskin clothes. Though they carry no muskets there is a bulge to their jackets where pistols are concealed. The two or three remaining Tory soldiers immediately jerk up their muskets at the "ready."*)

COTTON

(*Loudly.*)
Ground your arms!
(*The soldiers obey.*)

CAMPBELL

Well, Cousin Alec, you and your bodyguard are a little late for the festival. Or maybe you have come to the wedding.

MACALLISTER

No, I've not come to the wedding.
(*Dan Murchison walks next to Colonel MacAllister, and as he enters, Peggy rises half out of her seat and then sits quickly down again.*)

JENNIE BHAN

We don't want you here, Alec MacAllister, and the quicker you leave the better.

A Few Voices
(Somewhat threatening.)
Aye, we can do without you.

Other Voices
Down with the Whigs.

Cotton
What is your business, sir?

MacAllister
My business is legal enough and yours is not.

Cotton
(Hotly.)
I am a representative of the governor of this province.

MacAllister
North Carolina has no governor. Josiah Martin is a fugitive hiding on a ship at Wilmington and you know it.

Cotton
He is still the governor and will remain so until another is legally appointed by his majesty's government.

MacAllister
North Carolina has its own government and John Harvey is the head of it. And I have come as his representative to command you to disperse this gathering and every person to return quietly to his home and keep the peace.

Cotton
(*Sternly.*)
And you may consider yourself under arrest.
(*Several of the young fellows crowd protectingly around Colonel MacAllister, with their hands against their blouses.*)

MacAllister
(*Cooly.*)
And I do not. I hold prior appointment as a member of the Committee of Safety, signed by this same Josiah Martin himself, and I exercise that authority.
(*Turning to the people.*)
We are all neighbors together. I know most of you by sight. I have talked to you. You have heard me again and again warn you—

Jennie Bhan
Now he's starting to make a speech.

MacAllister
And I plead with you not to take up arms against the cause for which we stand.

Voice
Yea, we know—the cause of liberty. Down with him.

MacAllister
Liberty. And once more I say the same thing to you, Flora, and you, Allan. For God's sake at least remain neutral in this war that is coming, or you will be destroyed.

Allan
I am sorry, but we have chosen and you are no longer our friend.

MacAllister
Then you shall be treated as an enemy.
> (*Colonel Cotton is seen speaking to the clerk. The clerk rises and starts away at the left. One of the buckskin boys steps in front of him and stops him. MacAllister calls out.*)

Stop that man!

Colonel Cotton
Let him pass.

MacAllister
He'll stay here.
> (*Loudly to the people.*)

You all are dismissed.

Cotton
> (*Furiously.*)

You shall pay for this.

MacAllister
We'll all pay for it one way or another.

Cotton
I'll hang you high as Haman.

MacAllister
We'll see who gets hanged first. And now, I inform you that Generals Lillington and Caswell are camped beyond

the river with a Whig force. At the least sign of armed gathering in this town they will march upon it.

(*Murmurs of uneasiness break out among the people and some of them start moving away. Cotton suddenly sits down in his chair and stares before him, drumming on the table. The clerk quietly returns to his place. The organ begins its ominous and monotonous beat in the pedal again, and MacAllister and his escort turn as if to go back the way they came. Suddenly Dan runs across the scene over to Peggy and seizes her hand.*)

Dan

(*Vehemently.*)
It's going to be all right, Peggy. It is.
(*To those about him.*)
And when this war is over she and I together—
(*Donald springs forward and seizes him. With a cry almost of joy, Dan whirls upon him and knocks him down. Allan and several others move towards him, but the Whigs step between them, several of them pulling out their pistols. Donald climbs to his feet, jerks Colonel Cotton's sword from him, but is immediately disarmed by Fanning and others. Some of the people cry out with fear and many of them hurry out of the scene.*)

Donald

(*His face white with rage.*)
I'll—I'll have your life for this—I'll—

Jennie Bhan

You'll nothing, Donald. Let these fools alone. Get out of

my sight, Alec MacAllister. And you, Dan Murchison, the cut-throats that you are.

>   (*At this moment one of the soldiers, who had gone out with the Reverend John MacLeod, enters. He is much the worse for wear. His musket is gone, his clothes torn, and his face showing the signs of a fist fight.*)

SOLDIER

>   (*Running up to Colonel Cotton and panting out his words.*)

The minister! They've got him, sir. They've—

COTTON

What is it?

SOLDIER

They took my gun away from me. The Reverend MacLeod! The Whigs have carried him across the river.

MACALLISTER

Don't think we kidnapped the preacher. He's an old friend of ours who will spend a few days with us—

>   (*Bowing.*)

—whether he likes it or not. Well, Flora and Allan, we win the first skirmish and we'll win the last.

>   (*He bows again and goes out at the right with his men. The organ continues its accompaniment till they disappear.*)

COTTON

>   (*Suddenly springing up.*)

General MacDonald—

THE HIGHLAND CALL

(*To Donald.*)
—Captain, we must get to the governor at once.
(*To the people who are left.*)
Now to your homes, arm yourselves, and be ready to march against the Whigs at once. The war has come.
(*The light blacks out from the scene and comes up on the chorus as it rises and sings, the organ accompanying with a sort of cannonading ground bass beneath.*)

Chorus

Scots, wha ha'e wi' Wallace bled!
Scots, wham Bruce has aften led!
Welcome to your gory bed,
Or to victorie!
Now's the day and now's the hour;
See the front of battle lour!
See approach proud Edward's pow'r,
Chains and slaverie!

By oppressions, woes and pains!
By our sons in servile chains!
We will drain our dearest veins,
But they shall be free!
Lay the proud usurpers low!
Tyrants fall in every foe!
Liberty's in every blow!
Let us do, or die!

(*At the conclusion of the song the light fades out and comes up again on Mr. Mac.*)

Mr. Mac

And so up and down the valley the leaders of the two sides rallied their supporters. Colonel Moore, Lillington,

Ashe, Caswell, Harnett, and MacAllister on the Whig side, and Allan MacDonald, Colonel Cotton, Governor Martin, Colonel Donald MacLeod, Donald MacDonald, and others on the Tory. Now there was no turning back, and Flora MacDonald threw herself into the cause with all the energy and devotion of her nature. She became the leading spirit, the Joan of Arc, as it were, of the empire's cause. Day and night, unceasingly, she rode among her people, talking and persuading, making clear to them in burning terms the rightness of the loyalist side and the need now to rise in defense of their king. In the meantime, General Clinton and Sir Peter Parker had arrived in the Cape Fear River with their fleet and troops of British soldiers, and with such powerful aid assured, the Highlanders flocked to the king's standard, which had been raised at a central place near what is now Carthage, North Carolina. Soon an army of several thousand men was in the making.

On the Whig side enthusiasm grew upon enthusiasm. The news of Lexington, Bunker Hill, the taking of Boston, the raising of troops by General George Washington, the capturing of Montreal, and the report that Congress was now determined on actual separation from England rather than the simple righting of the colonists' wrongs, ran like wildfire among the Whigs everywhere, and they rallied on every muster ground. And Dan Murchison, now known for the daring spirit that was in him, was promoted a captain and sent to Averysboro and the eastern reaches of Cumberland to raise a company. As history would have it, Donald MacDonald was appointed by General MacDonald to the west of the valley to raise a company of Highlanders.

In Cross Creek the citizens, now fearing to be caught

THE HIGHLAND CALL 163

between two opposing fires, were scattering from the town. And Peggy MacNeill with old Sandy and Simey went back to her beloved Killiegrey, there to carry on farming as best they could and finish the house. The order came for the king's forces to march to Wilmington as a base of operations, and the Highland army set out with flags flying, pipes blowing, and Flora MacDonald cheering them on. The Whigs, on the watch, hurried to cut them off and with forced marches arrived at Moore's Creek Bridge ahead of them. And here was played out the drama between Dan Murchison and Donald MacDonald. An attack was ordered and in a few minutes was decided the fate of North Carolina and perhaps the fate of the empire itself. A great shout was raised for king and country and the dauntless Highlanders stormed over the bridge. But they were met by a rain of lead and artillery fire. Many of the leaders were killed at the first volley, and confusion spread among the ranks. In vain, Donald MacDonald, lying mortally wounded on the ground, tried to rally his comrades as they fled in every direction. Nearly a thousand of them were captured, among them being Allan MacDonald himself, his son Alexander, Major MacLeod, and Colonel Cotton.

In the following months scenes of great cruelty took place—comparable to those that Flora MacDonald had experienced among the clan wars in Scotland. Parties of Whigs roamed up and down the valley capturing scattered Tories, pillaging and burning their places and driving off their cattle. Fire and sword was the rule. But still Flora kept up the hopeless struggle to rally the remnants of the army and to free her husband and her son—

(*The light fades from Mr. Mac and comes up on the center stage.*)

SCENE 3

The interior of Flora MacDonald's home at Killiegrey. The room is a rather striking one in a frontier or backwoods manner. A rough table is at the center back. Over at the right front is a fireplace and on the wall above it a heavy-framed portrait of Prince Charlie. To the right rear is a door and to the left front another door. At the center back is a large window, with rich hanging curtains of the clan tartan. To the left of the window and spread out on the wall is a British flag. At the right of the left door is a portrait of Allan MacDonald and other MacDonald chieftains, dressed in their warlike regalia. A few antique Scottish chairs are scattered about. When the curtain rises Sandy Ochiltree is pacing back and forth with a musket. He is giving himself commands and awkwardly executing them. Seated on a bench at the window is Simey, dressed in full Indian garb. He wears a pack on his back.

SANDY

Parade rest.
  (*He does so.*)
Shoulder arms. Right about. Forward march.
  (*He marches a few steps.*)
To the rear march.
  (*He bangs the musket down on the floor and wipes his forehead with his sleeve.*)
Dang my soul if I can learn this stuff. What's the use of all these commands when a man's got nothing to do but aim and load and shoot?
  (*Commanding himself.*)
Ready, aim, fire—and all by the book.

THE HIGHLAND CALL

(*He does so, stamping the floor to give the shot. Then he consults the little book lying on the table.*)
And that was the trouble at Moore's Creek Bridge. Too many commands and not enough execution. Now here are the Whigs—
(*Indicating a place on the floor.*)
—and here are us Tories. We come a-marching up. "Lay down your arms!" we say. But they lie still and say nothing. Then what do we do? Form fours.—Form fours, men!—And we come walking into death with their bullets flying through the air? No sir. We scatter every man and jook behind trees and stay there until dark. Then we creep across the creek—
(*He does so.*)
—and up the bank and tear in on 'em with a dreadful cutting and chopping of blades.
(*He goes through some antics of stabbing the enemy, Simey stands up, grunts, and jerks his head towards the door. Sandy is now down on the floor savagely choking a Whig. He looks up at Simey.*)
Whist! We stay right here with Mistress Flora till the last trump. Take off that pack. You been wearing it for days. But we ain't gonna march away to the west I tell you. Not till—till—
(*There is a knock on the door at the left and then a hammering. Sandy stares around him terrified and calls out.*)
Who is it?

VOICE
(*Beyond the door.*)
Open up.

SANDY

(*Half-weeping.*)
I knowed it, I knowed it! Soon as they go off and leave me here guarding the house them Whigs would have to come again.

(*The hammering on the door continues.*)
Go away, go away. There's nobody here but me and poor old Simey. Go away.

VOICE

It's me—Colonel MacAllister. Open up. I'm not going to hurt you.

(*Finally Sandy goes over, unbars the door and opens it slightly.*)

SANDY

Uck—

MACALLISTER

(*Pushing his way in.*)
Where's your mistress?

SANDY

Sorrow and woe is our lot—Ochon—Ochrie! And only a handful of days is left to us.

MACALLISTER

What are you doing with that gun?

SANDY

Please, sir, just playing with it.

THE HIGHLAND CALL

MacAllister
Guarding the house, eh?

Sandy
In a manner of speaking—sir. But Lord protect us, there ain't much to guard. We hadn't more'n got the dreadful news from Moore's Creek about how Master Allan was made a prisoner and Master Alexander too, and poor Master Donald was killed in cold blood.

MacAllister
I know. Greetings, Simey.
(Simey stares coldly at him. Sandy goes on in a roll of words.)

Sandy
Aye, sir—and then up come the Whigs marching through the yard, and they driv off our cattle and me fighting valiant—like to the last breath. They taken our corn and they threatened to burn down our house and Mistress Peggy begging 'em on her knees not to! Ill-sick she was but still a-begging of 'em. Then they go away and another crowd comes in a week or two. They taken the silverware and what little meat we got in the smokehouse. And now you come—with your men.

MacAllister
I'm alone.
(Simey starts creeping up behind MacAllister, his tomahawk raised. Sandy springs across the room and jerks him back.)

Sandy

Ow-ow! He'd hang us all.
   (*Turning again to MacAllister.*)
Oh, say you won't harm poor mistress.

MacAllister

Of course not. Where is she?

Sandy

Down the hill there by the spring. They've gone to put the baby away.

MacAllister

Uhm. Anne's?

Sandy

Aye. The Whigs burnt down Major MacLeod's house and poor Mistress Anne had to move over here. Three weeks ago the first child was took sick and it died and we buried it down there, and yesterday the other one.
   (*Savagely.*)
May the curse of the forty-eight kings, including Fergus—

MacAllister

Never mind the curse—And they are burying the baby?

Sandy

And left me here to watch over the ruins of this house.

MacAllister

   (*Gazing about him.*)
The house looks all right.

THE HIGHLAND CALL

SANDY

But stripped, stripped worse'n the lady in the Bible. Oh, if I'd had a little help—

MACALLISTER

Some things they haven't stripped—that picture of Bonnie Prince Charlie there, and that flag.

SANDY

We had 'em hid, sir.

MACALLISTER

You better burn 'em up.
(*Sandy gets between MacAllister and the flag.*)
Have you any food left?

SANDY

Hardly a grain, sir. I swept the floor of the barn this morning to get a little corn and beat it up. We got a mush cooking there. Mistress Peggy has. But for her we would have starved long ago, we would. And Simey kills a squirrel now and then in the woods.
(*Pleadingly.*)
You didn't bring us any food, did you, sir?

MACALLISTER

No.

SANDY

Mis' Jennie brung us something yesterday—all the way from her mill she did. Kinsfolks ort to hold together, she said, Whig or Tory.

MACALLISTER

She's not here?

SANDY

Yes sir—down there helping put the little baby away. I dug its grave this morning. And when they come back, me and Simey got to go down there and cut logs and pile on 'em to keep the wolves from getting at 'em. Ah—
   (*He throws up his hands in a gesture, and his musket falls clattering to the floor. He whirls around in fright and stands trembling, then reaches gingerly down and picks the musket up.*)
Some day that thing's going to shoot and kill me sure as I'm born. It jumps right out of my hand.
   (*Peggy enters at the right rear.*)

MACALLISTER

How are you, Peggy?
   (*She comes hurrying over to him.*)

PEGGY

Cousin Alec—And Dan, have you news of him?

MACALLISTER

He's all right.

PEGGY

Every day I expect to hear something dreadful's happened.

MACALLISTER

   (*Consolingly.*)
Not to Dan Murchison. Any other man would have been killed long ago.

FLORA MACDONALD (*played by Margaret Holmes,* 1939 production) says farewell to her beloved home, Killiegrey

PEGGY
We heard about him leading the raid on Fort Johnston and almost capturing Governor Martin singlehanded!

MacAllister
If we had a thousand men like him we'd win this war in a month.

Peggy
And it will be ended soon, won't it?

MacAllister
We hope so.

Peggy
Sandy, go down in the hollow and 'tend to the goat and bring some milk for Miss Anne.
(*She hurries over to the fireplace and stirs the gruel.*)

Sandy
Aye, ma'am.

Peggy
And take your gun. Maybe you'll see a rabbit or a squirrel.

Sandy
I couldn't hit a barn door. Come on, Simey, bring your bow.

MacAllister
I'm sorry to hear about Anne's children.

PEGGY

It's almost killed her and Aunt Flora too.

MACALLISTER

Aye, Flora doted on her grandchildren and had great hopes for them.

PEGGY

(*Softly.*)
Hopes.

MACALLISTER

In this new country—
(*Shaking his head.*)
Ah, but I warned her, pleaded with her, but it did no good.

PEGGY

She saw her duty and has done it, and will keep on doing it.

MACALLISTER

Not likely now—she won't.

PEGGY

What's happened?
(*The door at the right opens, and Jennie Bhan, Flora, Anne, and James come in. Anne is crushed with grief, and the few months of suffering have left their mark on Flora. But she still walks with unbowed head. The pinch of poverty shows in their threadbare clothes.*)

THE HIGHLAND CALL

JENNIE BHAN
(*Suddenly stopping.*)
Well, more trouble!

MACALLISTER
(*Quietly.*)
Greetings—Flora—Anne—you too, Jamie.
(*They return his greetings.*)

PEGGY
(*Who has dipped some gruel into a bowl.*)
Come to your room, Anne. This will make you feel better.
(*She leads Anne out at the left.*)

FLORA
How are your people, Cousin Alec?

MACALLISTER
They are all well.

JENNIE BHAN
None of your boys been killed yet?

MACALLISTER
I hope not. And yours?

JENNIE BHAN
Ain't heard a word from 'em in this madness. Aye, the whole world's gone crazy. Here in this very house—Peggy working away at night knitting and making things to send to Dan Murchison wherever he might be. And Flora and Jamie and Anne weaving and sewing for Allan and Alexander shut tight there in Halifax.

####### MacAllister
And I reckon you knit one sock for a Whig and another'n for a Tory, being as you've got boys on both sides.

####### Jennie Bhan
Well, there's some sense in that. At least you do justice to both sides. Oh, I reckon they'll go on killing and shooting till there ain't nobody left. And what for? You and your liberty, and Flora here, poor thing, with her empire and her one great English-speaking race united.

####### James
I'll get some wood to cook supper, Mother.
(*He goes out and Jennie sits down near the fireplace and begins lighting her pipe.*)

####### MacAllister
And now, Flory, I want a final talk with you—

####### Flora
Final?

####### MacAllister
Before it's too late. The Whig leader, Colonel Alston, is marching down this way, burning and laying waste all Tory property.
(*Flora is silent.*)
I sent a fast messenger to Dan Murchison, urging him to meet me here quick as possible. Whether he'll arrive in time, I don't know.

THE HIGHLAND CALL

JENNIE BHAN
(*With a touch of bitterness.*)
Then the war grows crazier. You mean it'll be Whigs against Whigs, fighting over her?

MACALLISTER
I hope not. But fire and sword are loose, Flora, and this is no organized warfare in the Cape Fear Valley now, but a bloody civil war.

JENNIE BHAN
And you've been a ringleader in bringing it on, Alec MacAllister.

MACALLISTER
And Flory, I've come here to ask you to be sensible. Take the oath for the American cause, and thereby save yourself and your family.

FLORA
(*Turning to him, her voice strong and imperious.*)
This war is not ended yet. We have just begun to fight.

MACALLISTER
(*Staring at her.*)
Good God, you're out of your mind.

FLORA
It's true we lost the battle of Moore's Creek Bridge. But our people have shown their worth. The Highlanders are still fighting, and they will continue to fight, even in small bands, until the king has sent enough troops to beat you traitors to the earth and bring peace again. And I will

never, never take oath against the cause I believe in, against another oath I took long ago. It's right and I will stand with it until I die.

JENNIE BHAN

She's a stubborn Scot like you, Alec. You might know that.

MACALLISTER
(*Snapping.*)
But what will you do now?

FLORA

Continue to speak and work for the truth as I see it. You are wrong. Jefferson and Washington are wrong. Time will prove it. The people are not united against the king. The majority are for him. Your Congress in Philadelphia is divided. And already reinforcements are being sent to General Clinton on the Cape Fear.

MACALLISTER

How do you know that?

FLORA

Do you think I sit here idle every day and do nothing?

JENNIE BHAN

She's become a regular Paul Revere, riding out at night.

MACALLISTER

The British government has just recalled Clinton from the Cape Fear, Flora.

Flora
No!

MacAllister
He sailed to the north three days ago.
> (*Flora suddenly sits down in her chair and says nothing. The door opens and Peggy comes in again. MacAllister continues.*)

And now I'm to tell you that the North Carolina Assembly orders you to take this oath or—
> (*He pulls a document from his pocket.*)

Flora
(*Quietly.*)
I'll never sign it.

MacAllister
(*Angrily.*)
You'll sign it, Flory,—if it means life or death.

Flora
No.

Peggy
(*Coming forward.*)
Cousin Alec, they wouldn't do that. It's inhuman.

MacAllister
War is always inhuman.

Peggy
But you could stop them.

MacAllister

It is a law passed by the General Assembly and is beyond me now.

Peggy

You have power.

MacAllister

But no military authority in this matter.

Flora

(*Murmuring.*)
Killiegrey—it once had a meaning. It still has.
(*Suddenly crying out.*)
They'll not take it away from us. This is some mad dream. The king's men will come. Allan will be freed from prison, my boy will be freed, and we'll win this fight.

MacAllister

A mad dream, Flory? Then you are the dreamer. I am dealing in facts, hard facts. And I have come all this distance to give you a last chance to save yourself. Peggy here knows it and that's why she's on our side.

Flora

Peggy's lost her mind to Dan Murchison, that's why she's on your side. Some crazy quirk of destiny played it that way, and a bullet meant for somebody else killed Donald at Moore's Creek.

MacAllister

(*Vehemently.*)
But you can't stand out against us, Flory—We are—
(*Suddenly there is the sound of shots in the distance.*

THE HIGHLAND CALL

Peggy runs to the window at the rear and looks out. Jennie Bhan throws her knitting aside, springs up and grasps Sandy's musket. There is a scramble at the left and Sandy comes flying in, carrying a small bucket in his hand.)

SANDY

The Whigs coming down the road! They seen me and let fly a monstrous great volley. And look, they put a hole plumb through that bucket and all the milk's leaked out.

JENNIE BHAN

I tell you this, Alec MacAllister. If you let them Whigs come in here and do harm to Flora I'll kill somebody if it's the last thing I ever do.
(*Looking at the gun, then handing it quickly to Sandy.*)
Here, take your musket and go out and defend yourself like a man.

SANDY

(*Moaning as he takes it.*)
Oh, I would but there ain't no use—them frenzy-minded cut-throats—Ooh, listen at 'em. They're coming on like savage dogs, a-yelling and a-barking.
(*In the distance yells can be heard. Simey backs in at the left with his bow drawn. Sandy comes over and quiets him. Now in the adjoining room the sound of a woman's sobbing is heard.*)

JENNIE BHAN

And they're scaring poor Anne to death.
(*She goes out at the left. Sandy comes and sits down near the fire, bowing his head over against the mus-*

ket in his hands. Suddenly Peggy turns from the window to Flora.)

Peggy
(*Taking her by the arm.*)
Go upstairs and let me talk to them, please, Aunt Flora.
(*There is a trampling of feet outside and a thundering on the door. Peggy opens it. A rough-looking young corporal of some twenty-five or -six enters, grimy and splashed with mud. He carries a heavy sword in his hand. The voices of men talking outside are heard.*)
What do you want?

Corporal
(*Eyeing Colonel MacAllister and then saluting him.*)
We have orders for the arrest of one Flora MacDonald.
(*Bowing to Peggy.*)
Your servant, ma'am.

Peggy
By whose orders do you act?

Corporal
(*Grinning and showing his snaggled front teeth.*)
You might say by our own orders, but we do have a piece of paper from Colonel Alston. The lady is to be taken— Where is she?

MacAllister
This is the oath, Corporal, for her to sign.

Flora
I am Flora MacDonald.

Corporal
(*Bowing again.*)
Thanky ma'am.
(*Calling to the men outside.*)
Have the place searched!
(*Turning back.*)
And what's your name, ma'am?

Peggy
Peggy MacNeill.

Corporal
You're a purty thing. Whig or Tory?

Peggy
(*After an instant of silence.*)
I am for the Whig cause, sir, but Flora MacDonald is my aunt, and I'm for her too.

Corporal
Ah, but she's a traitor and I doubt not we shall see her hanged.
(*To Flora.*)
Now, ma'am, if you have any preparations, make 'em quick. And then everybody get out of the house, for it might prove a little warm here.

Peggy
Would you burn the place down?

CORPORAL

That is our intention.
(He looks about him and sees the flag. Snatching it down, he flings it on the table. James comes rushing in with an armful of wood. He stops, throws the wood toward the fireplace, and advances on the soldier.)

JAMES

Get out!
(Flora lays her hand on James's arm. Jennie Bhan comes in at the left with Anne.)

CORPORAL

Is he your son? We want him too. He's named in the paper.
(James springs across the room and seizes a piece of wood, but MacAllister hurries in front of him.)

MACALLISTER

Keep your head, boy.

JENNIE BHAN
(To the corporal.)
If I was a man I'd wring your neck.

CORPORAL
(Whirling around.)
Ah-hah, another Tory.

JENNIE BHAN

I'm not a Tory, but I'd like to get my broadsword and

cut your shirt off. Ain't you got no respect for people—busting into their houses like this?

CORPORAL

If you ain't a Tory what you doing here?

JENNIE BHAN

Helping out with the sick folks and the suffering. That's bigger than Whig or Tory. Of course you don't understand that.

CORPORAL

(*Soberly.*)
I reckon I do. Suffering, we all know what that is.
(*Snapping.*)
But I got my orders.

JENNIE BHAN

For mercy's sake, do something, Flory. Don't sit there like seeing a ghost from yonder world.
(*Flora sits staring ahead of her saying nothing.*)
And you, Alec, ain't you going to lift a hand to save her?

MACALLISTER

It's Colonel Alston's affair now, not mine. She could still swear for our side.

SANDY

(*By the fire, groaning and shaking.*)
This is the end. The end has come upon us at the last.

Jennie Bhan

So they've got you, Flory. Now I'd be sensible and swear—I would.

Flora

(*Her voice breaking almost in a moan.*)
I cannot.

Anne

(*Now speaking for the first time, almost weeping.*)
Please, Mother. Let's save ourselves. There's nothing we can do about it.

Peggy

Do, Aunt Flora.
    (*Suddenly the sound of hoofbeats comes flooding up to the door at the right. A voice is heard calling.*)

Voice

Halt, who goes there?
    (*The sound of another voice answers. The door at the right opens and Dan Murchison comes striding in. He is followed by two or three of the corporal's men.*)

Peggy

(*With a cry.*)
Dan!
    (*She flies to him and he holds her close in his arms and kisses her.*)

Jennie Bhan

Well, Dan Murchison, I hope I'm glad to see you.

SANDY

Ow!

DAN

(*Genially, though his face is haggard and worn from exposure and hard riding.*)
Greetings, Colonel MacAllister—
(*Taking off his cap.*)
And you, madam.
(*To the soldier.*)
Corporal.

CORPORAL

(*Saluting.*)
Captain Murchison.

DAN

I have orders from General Lillington. Colonel Alston's prisoners are in my charge.

CORPORAL

Very well, sir.

DAN

And the Colonel will meet your troop at the ford on Mountain Creek. He has important news for you.

CORPORAL

My orders were to fire the house too, sir.

DAN

I'll take the authority.

Corporal

Yes sir.
>(*He salutes, and he and his men go out at the left. Immediately the sound of tramping feet begins and the corporal's voice is heard giving his orders.*)

Peggy

(*Bringing a piece of bread from the cupboard.*)
Here, Dan, you must be starved.
>(*He takes it and begins to devour it.*)

Flora

(*Coldly.*)
And now, what do you wish of us, Dan Murchison?

Dan

I wish I could leave you to live here in peace, ma'am, but I cannot. You are to take the oath, you and your household, or leave. It is a hard verdict, but a just one. At least it saves you—
>(*He stops and bites his bread.*)

Jennie Bhan

From hanging?
>(*He nods.*)

James

(*Angrily.*)
And what's to become of all we've done here? Our house, our barns and fields?

MacAllister

They will be confiscated by the government and transferred to—As a member of the committee I shall determine who.

JAMES
If you take them from us, Cousin Alec, may God curse you for it!

FLORA
When peace is restored, Jamie lad, and we have won this war, we'll have them back again. And here we'll gather once more, your father and brothers, and we'll go on as we've started. Till then—in Wilmington we have friends—

DAN
I'm sorry, ma'am. But the orders say the oath, or lacking that you'll leave these shores.

PEGGY
Dan!

DAN
But surely you'll sign it now, ma'am, for we have already won this war. Read this, Colonel MacAllister.
(He pulls a paper from his pocket and hands it to the colonel who spreads it out and runs his eyes over it.)

COLONEL MACALLISTER
(Reading abstractedly, then light breaking over his face.)
Listen, Flora, everybody. "We therefore do solemnly

publish and declare that these united colonies are, and of a right ought to be, free and independent States."
(*Triumphantly.*)
They've done it. Congress has declared independence.

Jennie Bhan

Thank the Lord, thank the Lord for that anyhow, and the war will soon be ended.

Dan

It will. And everywhere the people are shouting for joy. Bells are being rung. Prayers of thanksgiving in the churches, bonfires lit across the land. Last night Cross Creek was a blaze of light. Your stepfather himself, ma'am, joined in the parade. And everywhere the Tories are laying down their arms, deserting their cause—Ah, Peggy.
(*He puts his arm around her.*)

MacAllister

Read it, Flory, here.
(*He hands the document to her. She sits staring at it dully. Anne comes over to her and puts her arms around her.*)

Anne

Please, Mother, there's nothing more we can do. Let us stay here, keep our home.

James

Please, Mother.
(*They stand on either side of her.*)

FLORA
(*Gazing before her.*)
So with these words and these deeds you destroy our dream. Ah, more than that, the hopes of the world. And you, Alec MacAllister, Dan Murchison and Peggy, your children's children and their children will see some day how wrong you've been. In my heart I know it. And because I know it I'll stand true to the belief that's in me. They say swear obedience to this or take the consequences. I'll take the consequences.
(*She grinds the document in her hand and throws it on the floor, then rises out of her seat and speaks, as if to an unseen listener.*)
You'll see the meaning of this liberty—how the states will quarrel among themselves, civil war will be bred and the land overrun, how the rich will oppress the poor because they'll have the power to do it. How greed and avarice will flourish, waste and confusion, because they are free to. And the voice of the people will be bought and sold like cattle in the marketplace. And the land will be gutted and ruined and the treasures of the mountains and the forests rooted up as if by swine—and this nation of liberty and free men you talk of will become a land of demagogues and office seekers and bloated slave drivers. And so it's ended now. All the old days are ended. And what might have been a great and glorious empire of English men and women is broken and destroyed by these madmen. And for me and mine there's nothing to do now but to deny this land and turn our faces back to the old world—there to—die.
(*Shaking her head.*)
I'll get my shawl, Dan Murchison—Jamie—Anne.
(*She turns and goes out at the right, followed by*

James and Anne. Colonel MacAllister picks the document up from the floor.)

JENNIE BHAN
(*Half-weeping.*)
Her heart is broken, this day it is.
(*Angrily.*)
For what you've done tonight, Alec MacAllister, I would say God blast ye, but it ain't no use.

MACALLISTER
Not now.
(*Tapping the document in his hand.*)
Our cause has triumphed. Justice has won.

JENNIE BHAN
Justice—ah—

PEGGY
(*Holding to Dan's arm.*)
I can't stand it, her face. To see her look like that.

DAN
Nothing can be done about it, nothing. She won't give in.

PEGGY
Hearing her talk like that about the future—for a moment it almost frightened me. She seemed like a—like a sort of prophet seeing far ahead—

DAN
She's suffered so. And she's wrong, that's why she's suf-

fered. From the beginning she was wrong and her words were wrong. Ah, Peggy, it had to be like this—the weak had to give way and the wrong ideas had to give way. It is cruel but it's so—and it won't be like she said—
(*Fiercely.*)
—my country won't. We'll build it different—out of her very tears we'll build it—into something great and wonderful.
(*He holds Peggy tightly to him.*)

MacAllister

(*Jubilantly.*)
Aye, lad, we will. Mistakes will occur—like she said—evil things will happen, but the glory of it—and what she'll never see—is that we ourselves have the power to change these mistakes—to wipe out these evils—to make our country what we want it—
(*Staring before him.*)
Aye, that's it—we ourselves—free men—like this document says—and responsible men—both to ourselves and the generations that come after us—responsible in the terms of that very freedom. We must never forget that, and our children must never forget.
(*His strong and vibrant voice booming through the room as he stares ahead.*)
Yea with these living words and these deeds we begin *our* empire, Dan Murchison and Peggy MacNeill—an empire not of oppression and hate and power spreading over the world, but of justice, courage, and peace among men—And in the symbol of you two like our young country beginning—
(*His voice dies out and he gazes a moment at the floor.*)

Jennie Bhan
(*Shaking her head.*)
Listening to Flora there—for a minute seemed like she was right. And now seeing you, Dan and Peggy, standing there with the light on you, looking so fresh and young and hopeful—seems like you're right. Yes, maybe you are. Anyhow, I hope so.

Dan
And we are right.

MacAllister
Aye. Good night, Jennie Bhan. I must hurry back to Barmore.
   (*He turns and holds his hand out to her. With slothful reluctance she takes it and then begins flurriedly sweeping the hearth. MacAllister goes to the door.*)
Get them safely aboard ship in Wilmington, Dan. Even in her defeat I respect her.

Dan
I will, sir.
   (*MacAllister goes out and closes the door.*)

Jennie Bhan
(*Looking up at Sandy and Simey who are standing over at the left.*)
And what'll happen to you now, Sandy? Will you and Simey be going back in all your bravery across the raging water?

Sandy
We will not.
   (*Shuddering.*)

Simey won't cross them waters again—he won't—and we can't help pore Mistress now.
(*Simey grunts.*)
Yeah, we'll go. Tomorrow we will, him with his bow and arrows and me with my old musket. We been talking 'bout it for weeks now. To the west, over the mountains, clean away from all this. There among the Indians we'll live, with the prairie dogs and buffalo and forget all this, forget all this, and be free, really free.

JENNIE BHAN
Well, dang it, you may be right.

SANDY
And we are right.
(*Staring off.*)
First they make our mark and swear us fast, then write us down in a great book forever, and finally—who knows? —There, maybe by a river rolling from the great Pacific Mountains down they'll put us up a monument and cut our name in the 'mortality of everlasting stone—"Sandy and Simey Ochiltree of the Clan Ochiltree, first pioneers in the building of the west. There they sleep side by side." Ah, Simey boy, the wonder of it.
(*Flora comes in at the right rear with a shawl over her head, carrying a little bundle under her arm. Following her are Anne and James.*)

FLORA
We are ready, Dan.

DAN
I have some horses brought up to the road there.

Sandy
Good-by, Mistress, Mistress—good-by.

Flora
Thank you, Sandy. I leave this to you, Peggy and Dan. Killiegrey is yours.

Peggy
No, we don't want it, Aunt Flora. No.

Flora
And here, where we would have lived, you must live. There is a laurel bush I planted by the spring. See that it lives.

Peggy
(*Weeping.*)
Yes, yes.

Anne
(*Suddenly seizing Peggy's arm.*)
And the graves, Peggy. My children—care for them.
(*Peggy nods her head.*)

Dan
Aye.
(*They all go out at the left front, Dan and Peggy going last.*)

Jennie Bhan
(*In a sudden stir as she is left alone.*)
I won't stay here another night.
(*She lifts the gruel from the fire and flings down the poker.*)

I'm going with you—far as home.

(*She hurries out after them. For a moment the stage is empty and silent, save for one long calling note in the organ. The keening begins in the chorus and Flora reappears in the door. She gazes heavily about the room, then at the portrait above the fireplace, the while she abstractedly picks up the flag and holds it to her. The keening grows louder, and for an instant the secret of her long-ago love for Bonnie Prince Charlie is revealed in the farewell of her face. She gazes about her once more, and then goes swiftly away, leaving the door wide open. The keening swells into a final crescendo, and with a great swirl of rising organ chords, the scene fades out and the lights come on in the theatre.*)

THE END

THE HIGHLAND CALL SONGBOOK

THE HIGHLAND CALL SONGBOOK

I. MUSIC IN THE PLAY:

Organ Overture (Act One) *Charles Vardell*	205
Flora MacDonald's Lament *Sung by the Chorus*	211
O God, Our Help in Ages Past *Sung by the Chorus*	212
Wae's Me for Prince Charlie *Sung by the Chorus*	213
The Gay Young Widow *Sung by Sandy Ochiltree*	215
The Highland Widow's Lament *Hummed by the chorus and actors*	216
Hail to the Chief *Sung by the Chorus*	217
Fareweel, O, Fareweel *Sung by the Chorus*	218
I Wish I Were Where Helen Lies *Sung by Peggy MacNeill*	219
Organ Overture (Act Two) *Charles Vardell*	221
By Yon Bonnie Banks *Hummed by the chorus*	228
Jennie Bhan's Lullaby *Sung by Jennie Bhan MacNeill*	229

THE HIGHLAND CALL

    O, Gilderoy Was a Bonnie Boy   230
      Sung by Sandy Ochiltree

    The Bonnie Earl of Murray   232
      Sung by Sandy Ochiltree

    God Save the King   233
      Sung by the chorus and actors

    The Highland Fling   234
      Danced by the Flora MacDonald Girls

    Polwart on the Green   235
      Danced by the Flora MacDonald Girls

    Scots Wha Ha'e Wi' Wallace Bled   236
      Sung by the Chorus

II. OTHER OLD CAPE FEAR VALLEY FAVORITES—being a cross section of bagpipe tunes, chants, children's songs, dances, fiddling pieces, folk ballads, carols, folksongs, hymn tunes, and patriotic pieces collected by Mr. Mac, selected and reprinted here from his scrapbook:

    Accuse Me Not   237
      Sung by Donald MacDonald, aided on the spinet

    All Is Well   238
      Favorite of Hector MacNeill

    Babylon Is Fallen   239
      Old Bluff Church favorite

    Bannocks O' Bear-meal   239
      A dancing tune

    Barbara Allan   240
      Cornelius Harnett's special ballad

THE HIGHLAND CALL	201
The Bush Aboon Traquair	242
Ca' the Yowes to the Knowes *Lassies' spinning song*	243
Come O'er the Stream, Charlie	244
Early One Morning *A favorite of Anne MacLeod*	245
The Earth Belongs Unto the Lord *Old Longstreet favorite*	246
Eternal Father, Strong to Save	247
Good-Morrow, 'Tis St. Valentine's Day *Taught to the young ladies of Fayetteville by Llewellyn Lechmere Wall, a traveling actor*	248
Green Grow'th the Holly *A favorite Christmas carol*	249
The Hawthorne and the Maid *An especial favorite of Mr. Mac, the words fitted by him to the tune of "Ye Banks and Braes o' Bonnie Doon" or "The Caledonian Hunt's Delight"*	250
Heart's-Ease *A favorite of Farquhar Campbell, that gay sport*	252
How Should I Your True Love Know? *Made popular in Fayetteville by Mrs. Herndon, the actress, when she and her husband appeared there in 1795 at the Drury Lane Theatre in such pieces as "Antidote for the Spleen," "The Country Girl," and "A Peep into the Seraglio"*	253

I Loathe That I Did Love   253
Another of Mr. Wall's pieces, taught to Colonel MacAllister, who sang it in his declining years, his Negro boy Hannibal accompanying him on the guitar

In Sad and Ashy Weeds   254
Sung by Mr. Herndon

John Anderson, My Jo   255
A favorite of old scrubblin Archibald MacNeill, Jennie Bhan's husband

The Lord At First Did Adam Make   256
An old Cameron Hill favorite

Lord Gregory   257
Another of Mr. Mac's special pieces, and to be quavered forth by him when you catch him in the mood

The Man That Lives Must Learn to Die   258
Old Barbecue favorite

My Love Was Born in Aberdeen   259
A dance tune

O Mortal Man, Remember Well   260
A favorite of the Reverend Mr. MacLeod

The Romish Lady   261
Beloved by the sisters of old Bluff Church

The Spanish Lady   263
Sung by Farquhar Campbell's male quartet

Take, Oh, Take Those Lips Away   264
Sung by Mrs. Herndon

THE HIGHLAND CALL 203

There Was a Lady Loved a Swine 265
Sung by Jennie Bhan MacNeill to her children

The Three Ravens 266
Sung by Farquhar Campbell with his lute

Tomorrow Shall Be My Dancing Day 268
A favorite of young Flora Murchison, daughter of Dan Murchison and his wife Peggy, who died of the fever at the age of seventeen and lies buried in an unmarked grave there across the creek from Cool Spring

'Twas on That Dark, That Doleful Night 269
Old Bethesda hymn

The Twelve Blessings of Mary 270
Sung by Jennie Bhan MacNeill to her children

Westron Wind 270
Sung by Farquhar Campbell to his lute and to his cronies

When Maggie and I Was Acquaint 272
Old Hugh MacDonald's favorite

ORGAN OVERTURE (ACT ONE)

Charles Vardell

Chorus "Flora Macdonald's Lament (in G) to follow immediately

FLORA MACDONALD'S LAMENT

James Hogg (1770-1835) — Neil Gow

Far over yon hills o' the heather sae green, And down by the corrie that sings by the sea, The bonnie young Flora sat sighing her lane, The dew on her plaid and the tear in her e'e. She looked at a boat wi' the breezes that swung, Away on the waves like a bird on the main; And aye as it lessen'd she sigh'd as she sung, "Fareweel to the lad I shall ne'er see again! Fareweel to my hero, the gallant and young, Fareweel to the lad I shall ne'er see again!"

The target is torn from the arm of the just,
The helmet is cleft on the brow of the brave,
The claymore for ever in darkness must rust,
But red is the sword of the stranger and slave.
The hoof of the horse and the foot of the proud,
Have trod o'er the plumes on the bonnet of blue;
Why slept the red bolt in the breast of the cloud
When tyranny revell'd in blood of the true?
"Fareweel my young hero, the gallant and good!
The crown of thy fathers is torn from thy brow!"

O GOD, OUR HELP IN AGES PAST

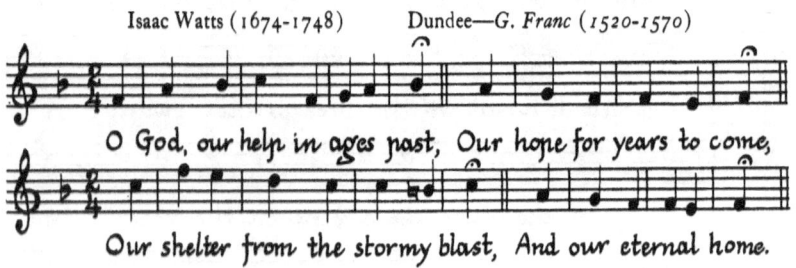

Isaac Watts (1674-1748)   Dundee—*G. Franc (1520-1570)*

O God, our help in ages past, Our hope for years to come,
Our shelter from the stormy blast, And our eternal home.

Time, like an ever rolling stream,
Bears all its sons away;
They fly, forgotten, as a dream
Dies at the opening day.

Before the hills in order stood,
Or earth received her frame,
From everlasting Thou art God,
To endless years the same.

WAE'S ME FOR PRINCE CHARLIE

Quoth I, "My bird, my bonnie, bonnie bird,
Is that a sang ye borrow,
Are these some words ye've learned by heart,
Or a lilt o' dool and sorrow?"
"Oh! no, no, no," the wee bird sang,
"I've flown sin' mornin' early,
But sic a day o' wind an' rain—
Oh! wae's me for Prince Charlie!

"On hills that are, by right, his ain,
He roves a lanely stranger,
On ev'ry side he's press'd by want,
On ev'ry side is danger.
Yestreen I met him in a glen,
My heart maist burstit fairly,
For sadly changed indeed was he—
Oh! wae's me for Prince Charlie!

"Dark night cam on, the tempest roar'd
Loud o'er the hills an' valleys,
An' where was't that your Prince lay down,
Wha's hame should been a palace?
He row'd him in a Highland plaid,
That cover'd him but sparely,
An' slept beneath a bush o' broom—
Oh! wae's me for Prince Charlie!"

But now the bird saw some red coats,
An' he shook his wings wi' anger,
"Oh! this is no a land for me;
I'll tarry-here nae langer!"
He hover'd on the wing a while
Ere he departed fairly,
But weel I mind the fareweel strain
Was "Wae's me for Prince Charlie!"

THE GAY YOUNG WIDOW

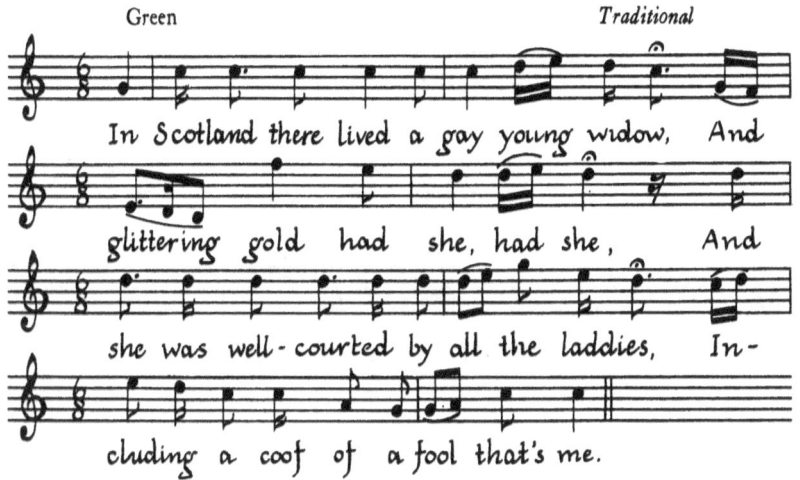

In Scotland there lived a gay young widow,
And glittering gold had she, had she,
And she was well-courted by all the laddies,
Including a coof of a fool that's me.

Her hair it was black, her eyes were sparkling,
Her lips they were ripe and red, so red,
And weary the hours I watched by her window
With an aching heart and woeful head.

At last she had pity on my sorrow,
And opened her shutter wide, so wide,
And flung in my face a pan of dishwater—
"How's that for a kiss?" the gay hussy cried.

THE HIGHLAND WIDOW'S LAMENT

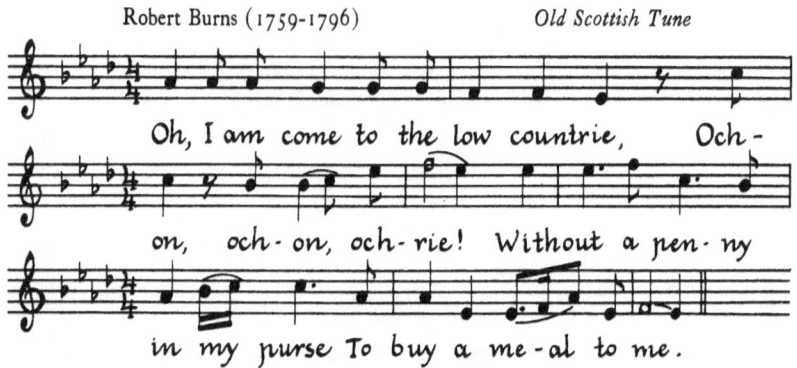

Robert Burns (1759-1796) Old Scottish Tune

Oh, I am come to the low countrie, Och-on, och-on, och-rie! Without a penny in my purse To buy a meal to me.

It was nae sae in the Highland hills,
  Ochon, ochon, ochrie!
Nae woman in the country wide
  Sae happy was as me.

For then I had a score o' kye,
  Ochon, ochon, ochrie!
Feeding on yon hills so high,
  And giving milk to me.

And there I had three score o' yowes,
  Ochon, ochon, ochrie!
Skipping on yon bonnie knowes,
  And casting wool to me.

I was the happiest of the clan,
  Sair, sair may I repine;
For Donald was the brawest lad,
  And Donald he was mine.

Till Charlie Stewart cam at last,
  Sae far to set us free;
My Donald's arm was wanted then,
  For Scotland and for me.

Their waefu' fate what need I tell,
  Right to the wrang did yield:
My Donald and his country fell
  Upon Culloden field

  Oh! I am come to the low countrie,
    Ochon, ochon, ochrie!
  Nae woman in the world wide
    Sae wretched now as me.

HAIL TO THE CHIEF

Ours is no sapling chance sown by the fountain,
  Blooming in Beltane, in winter to fade,
When the whirlwind has stript every leaf on the mountain,
  The more shall Clan Alpine exult in her shade.
    Moored in the rifted rock,
    Proof to the tempest shock,
  Firmer he roots him the ruder it blows—
    Monteith and Breadalbin' then
    Echo his praise again,
  Roderich Vich Alpine dhu ho! ieroe!

FAREWEEL, O, FAREWEEL

His staff's at the wa',
Toom, toom is his chair,
The bannet and a'
And I maun be here.
But O, he's at rest,
Where hearts ne'er were sair,
O to meet him again,
To part never mair.

I WISH I WERE WHERE HELEN LIES

Curst be the heart that thought the thought,
And curst the hand that fired the shot,
When in my arms burd Helen dropt,
    And died to succor me!

As I went down the water side,
None but my foe to be my guide,
None but my foe to be my guide,
    On fair Kirconnel lee.

I lighted down my sword to draw,
I hacked him in pieces sma',
I hacked him in pieces sma',
    For her sake that died for me.

O Helen fair beyond compare,
I'll make a garland of thy hair,
Shall bind my heart forever mair,
    Until the day I dee.

O that I were where Helen lies!
Night and day on me she cries;
Out of my bed she bids me rise,
    Says, "Haste and come to me."

I wish my grave were growing green,
A winding sheet o'er both my een,
And I in Helen's arms lying,
    On fair Kirconnel lee.

    I wish I were where Helen lies!
    Night and day on me she cries;
    And I am weary of the skies,
        For her sake that died for me.

ORGAN OVERTURE (ACT TWO)

Charles Vardell

Note: If the organ hasn't a standard pedal-board the high D's in the pedal part may be played an octave lower or omitted.

BY YON BONNIE BANKS

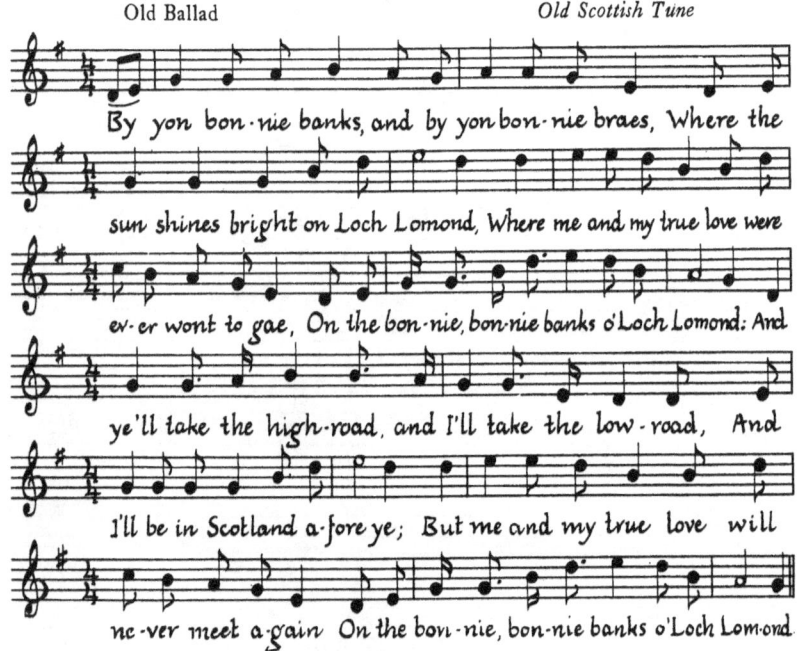

We'll meet where we parted in yon shady glen,
On the steep, steep side o' Ben Lomond,
Where in purple hue the Hielands we view,
And the moon looks out from the gloaming.

And ye'll take the high-road, etc.

O brave Charlie Stuart! dear to the true heart,
Who could refuse thee protection?
Like the weeping birch on the wild hillside,
How graceful he looked in dejection!

And ye'll take the high-road, etc.

The wild birdies sing, and the wild flowers spring,
And in sunshine the waters are sleeping;
But the broken heart it kens no second spring,
Though the woeful may cease from their greeting.

And ye'll take the high-road, etc.

JENNIE BHAN'S LULLABY

Trans. from the Gaelic by Malcolm MacFarlane *Ancient Lochaber Lullaby*

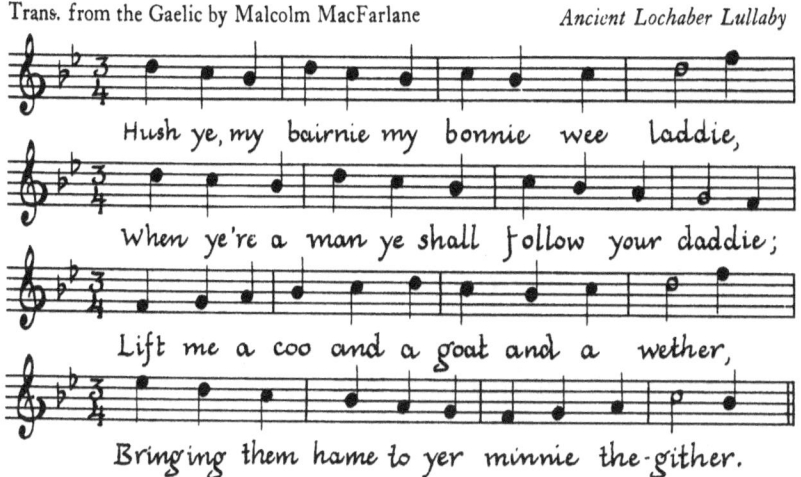

Hush ye, my bairnie my bonnie wee laddie,
When ye're a man ye shall follow your daddie;
Lift me a coo and a goat and a wether,
Bringing them hame to yer minnie the-gither.

Hush, ye, my bairnie, my bonnie wee lammie;
Routh o' guid things ye shall bring tae yer mammie;
Hare frae the meadow, and deer frae the mountain,
Grouse frae the muir lan', and trout frae the fountain.

Hush ye, my bairnie, my bonnie wee dearie,
Sleep! come and close the een heavy and wearie;
Closed are the wearie een, rest ye are takin',
Sound be yer sleepin', and bright be yer wakin'.

O, GILDEROY WAS A BONNIE BOY

17th Century Ballad

O, Gilderoy was a bonnie boy, Had roses till his shoon;
His stockings were of silken soy, Wi' garters hanging down. It was, I ween, a comely sight, To see sae trim a boy; He was my joy and heart's delight, My handsome Gilderoy. — (— hm —) — — — —

Oh! sike twa charming een he had,
A breath as sweet as rose,
He never ware a Highland plaid,
But costly silken clothes;
He gain'd the luve of ladies gay,
Nane eir tull him was coy;
Ah! wae is me! I mourn the day
For my dear Gilderoy.

Wi' mickle joy we spent our prime,
Till we were baith sixteen,
And aft we past the langsome time,
Among the leaves sae green;
Aft on the banks we'd sit us thair,
And sweetly kiss and toy,
Wi' garlands gay wad deck our hair
My handsome Gilderoy.

And when of me his leave he tuik,
The tears they wat mine ee,
I gave tull him a parting luik,
"My benison gang wi' thee;
God speed thee weil, mine ain dear heart,
For gane is all my joy;
My heart is rent sith we maun part,
My winsome Gilderoy."

Wae worth the loun that made the laws
To hang a man for gear,
To 'reave of life for ox or ass,
For sheep, or horse, or mare:
Had not their laws been made sae strick,
I neir had lost my joy,
Wi' sorrow neir had wat my cheek,
For my dear Gilderoy.

Of Gilderoy sae fraid they were,
They bound him mickle strong,
Tull Edenburrow they led him thair,
And on the gallows hung:
They hung him high aboon the rest,
He was sae trim a boy;
Thair dyed the youth whom I lued best,
My handsome Gilderoy.

THE BONNIE EARL OF MURRAY

He was a braw gallant,
And he played at the ba';
And the bonnie Earl o' Murray
Was the flower among them a'.
He was a braw gallant,
And he played at the gluve;
And the bonnie Earl o' Murray,
O he was the queen's luve.

O long will his lady look, etc.

GOD SAVE THE KING

Henry Carey (1692-1743)

God save our Lord the King, Long live our noble King, God save the King. Send him victorious, Happy and glorious, Long to reign over us, God save the King.

O Lord, our God, arise,
Scatter his enemies,
   And make them fall.
Confound their politics,
Frustrate their knavish tricks,
On thee our hopes we fix,
   God save us all.

Thy choicest gifts in store,
On him be pleased to pour,
   Long may he reign.
May he defend our laws,
And ever give us cause,
To sing with heart and voice,
   God save the King.

THE HIGHLAND FLING

Old Bagpipe Tune

POLWART ON THE GREEN

Allan Ramsay (1686-1758)   *Old Tune*

At Polwart on the green, If you'll meet me the morn, Where lassies do convene, To dance about the thorn; A kindly welcome you shall meet Frae her wha likes to view A lover and a lad complete, The lad and lover you.

Let dorty dames say, na,
As long as e'er they please,
Seem caulder than the snow,
While inwardly they bleeze:
But I will gravely show my mind,
And yield my heart to thee:
Be ever to the captive kind,
That longs na to be free.

SCOTS, WHA HA'E WI' WALLACE BLED!

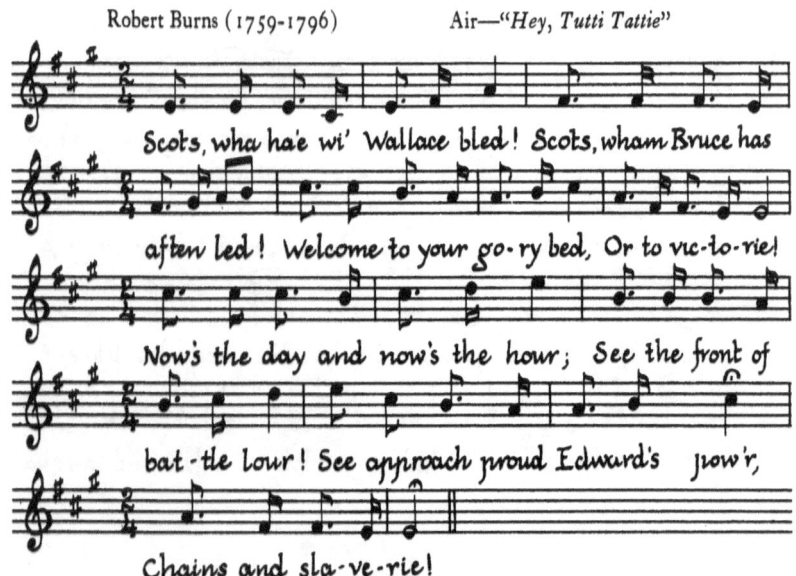

Robert Burns (1759-1796)   Air—"*Hey, Tutti Tattie*"

Scots, wha hae wi' Wallace bled! Scots, wham Bruce has aften led! Welcome to your gory bed, Or to victorie!
Now's the day and now's the hour; See the front of battle lour! See approach proud Edward's pow'r,
Chains and slaverie!

By oppression's woes and pains!
By your sons in servile chains!
We will drain our dearest veins,
But they shall be free!
Lay the proud usurpers low!
Tyrants fall in every foe!
Liberty's in every blow!
Let us do, or die!

ACCUSE ME NOT

Robert Tannahill   Air—"*She Rose and Let Me In*"

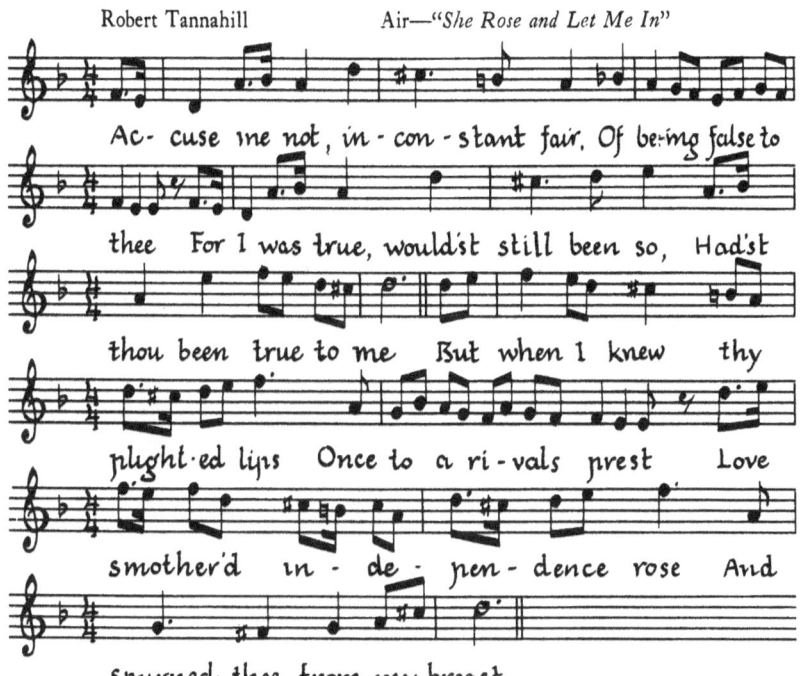

Ac-cuse me not, in-con-stant fair, Of being false to thee For I was true, would'st still been so, Hadst thou been true to me But when I knew thy plight-ed lips Once to a ri-vals prest Love smother'd in-de-pen-dence rose And spurned thee from my breast.

> The fairest flower in nature's field,
>   Conceals the rankling thorn,
> For thou, sweet flower! as false as fair,
>   This once kind heart hast torn.
> 'Twas mine to prove the fellest pangs,
>   That slightest love can feel.
> 'Tis thine to weep that one rash act,
>   Which bids this long farewell.

ALL IS WELL

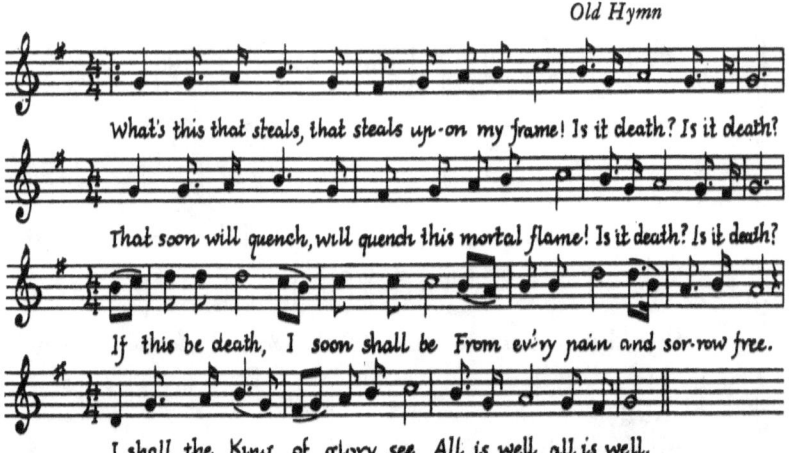

Old Hymn

What's this that steals, that steals up-on my frame! Is it death? Is it death?
That soon will quench, will quench this mortal flame! Is it death? Is it death?
If this be death, I soon shall be From ev'ry pain and sor-row free.
I shall the King of glory see, All is well, all is well.

    Weep not my friends, my friends, weep not for me.
        All is well, all is well.
    My sins forgiv'n, forgiv'n and I am free,
        All is well, all is well.
    There's not a cloud that doth arise,
    To hide my Jesus from my eyes.
    I soon shall mount the upper skies,
        All is well, all is well.

BABYLON IS FALLEN

rise no more.

BANNOCKS O' BEAR-MEAL

Bannocks o' bear-meal, and bannocks o' barley,
Here's to the Highland man's bannocks o' barley!
Wha in his days were loyal to Charlie?
Wha but the lads wi' the bannocks o' barley?

BARBARA ALLAN

O slowly, slowly went she up,
To the place where he was lyin',
And when she drew the curtain by,
"Young man, I think ye're dyin'."

"It's oh, I'm sick, I'm very very sick,
And it's a' for Barbara Allan;
O, the better for me ye'se never be
Though your heart's bluid were a-spillin'."

"O, dinna ye mind, young man," she said,
"When ye was in the tavern a-drinkin',
That ye made the healths gae round and round,
And slichtit Barbara Allan."

"He turn'd his face unto the wa',
And death was with him dealin';
Adieu, adieu, my dear friends a',
And be kind to Barbara Allan."

And slowly, slowly rase she up,
And slowly, slowly left him,
And sighin', said, she could not stay,
Since death of life had reft him.

She hadna gane a mile but twa,
When she heard the deid-bell ringin',
And every jow the deid-bell gi'ed,
It cried, "Wae to Barbara Allan."

"Oh, mother, mother, mak' my bed,
And mak' it saft and narrow;
Since my love died for me today
I'll die for him tomorrow."

THE BUSH ABOON TRAQUAIR

R. Crawford — Old Tune

Hear me ye nymphs, and ev'ry swain, I'll tell how Peggy grieves me; Though thus I languish and complain, Alas she ne'er believes me. My vows and sighs, like silent air, Unheeded never move her; The bonnie bush aboon Traquair, Was where I first did meet her.

That day she smiled and made me glad,
No maid seemed ever kinder;
I thought myself the luckiest lad,
So sweetly there to find her.
    I tried to soothe my amorous flame,
    In words that I thought tender;
    If more there passed, I'm not to blame,
    I meant not to offend her.

Yet now she scornful flies the plain,
The fields we then frequented;
If e'er we meet she shows disdain,
And looks as ne'er acquainted.
    The bonnie bush bloomed fair in May,
    Its sweets I'll aye remember;
    But now her frowns make it decay,
    It fades as in December.

CA' THE YOWES TO THE KNOWES

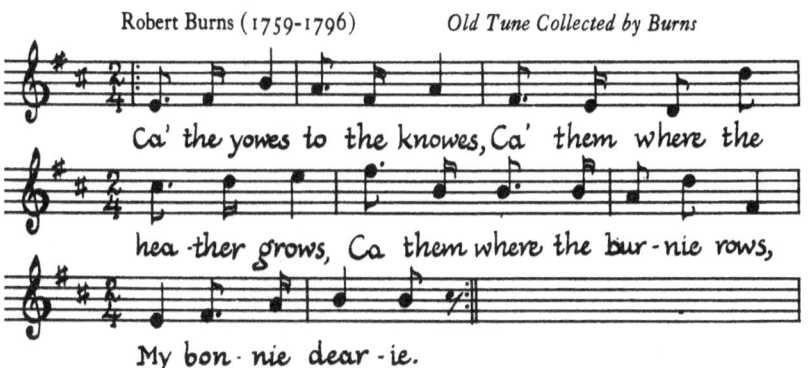

Robert Burns (1759-1796) Old Tune Collected by Burns

Ca' the yowes to the knowes, Ca' them where the hea-ther grows, Ca' them where the bur-nie rows, My bon-nie dear-ie.

Hark, the mavis' evening sang,
Sounding Cluden's woods amang,
Then a-faulding let us gang,
  My bonnie dearie.

Ca' the yowes to the knowes, etc.

We'd gang down by Cluden's side,
Through the hazels spreading wide,
O'er the waves that sweetly glide,
  To the moon sae clearly.

Ca' the yowes to the knowes, etc.

Yonder Cluden's silent tow'rs,
Whereat moonshine midnight hours,
O'er the dewy bending flowers,
  Fairies dance sae cheerie.

Ca' the yowes to the knowes, etc.

Fair and lovely as thou art,
Thou hast stown my very heart,
I can die but canna part,
  My bonnie 'earie.

Ca' the yowes to the knowes, etc.

COME O'ER THE STREAM, CHARLIE

Words after James Hogg *Old Highland Air*

Come o'er the stream, Charlie, dear Charlie, brave Charlie, Come o'er the stream, Charlie, And dine wi' Mac-Lean; And though you be wear-y, we'll make your heart cheer-y, And wel-come our Charlie and his roy-al train. We'll bring down the red deer, we'll bring down the black steer, The lamb from the bracken, and doe from the glen; The salt sea we'll har-ry, and bring to our Charlie, The cream from the bot-hy and curd from the pan.

Come o'er the stream, Charlie, etc.
And you shall drink freely the dews of Glen Sheerly,
That stream in the starlight where kings dinna ken;
And deep be your meed o' the wine that is red. . . .
To drink to your sire and his friend the MacLean.

Come o'er the stream, Charlie, etc.
If aught will invite you, or more will delight you,
'Tis ready—a troop of our bold Highlandmen
Shall range on the heather, wi' bonnet and feather,
Strong arms and broad claymores, three hundred and ten.

EARLY ONE MORNING

19th Century

Early one morning, just as the sun was rising, I heard a maid sing in the valley below: "O don't deceive me! O, never leave me! How could you use a poor maiden so?"

"O, gay is the garland, and fresh are the roses
I've culled from the garden to bind on thy brow.
  "O, don't deceive me, etc."

"Remember the vows that you made to your Mary,
Remember the bower where you vowed to be true?
  "O, don't deceive me, etc."

Thus sung the poor maiden, her sorrow bewailing,
Thus sung the poor maid in the valley below.
  "O, don't deceive me, etc."

ETERNAL FATHER, STRONG TO SAVE 247

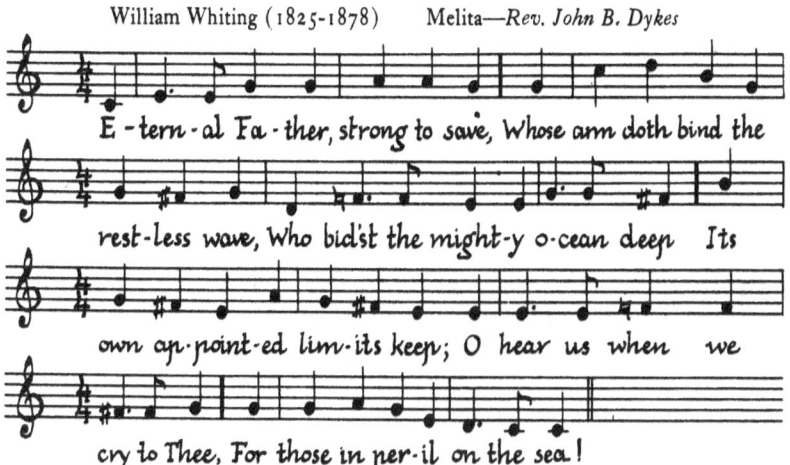

William Whiting (1825-1878) Melita—*Rev. John B. Dykes*

E-ternal Father, strong to save, Whose arm doth bind the restless wave, Who bid'st the mighty ocean deep Its own appointed limits keep; O hear us when we cry to Thee, For those in peril on the sea!

O Saviour, whose almighty word,
The winds and waves submissive heard,
Who walked'st on the foaming deep,
And calm amid its rage didst sleep;
O hear us when we cry to Thee
For those in peril on the sea!

O sacred Spirit, who did'st brood
Upon the chaos dark and rude,
Who bad'st its angry tumult cease,
And gavest light, and life, and peace;
O hear us when we cry to Thee
For those in peril on the sea!

GOOD-MORROW, 'TIS ST. VALENTINE'S DAY

Cf. Ophelia's Song in *Hamlet*   Air—*"Lord Thomas and Fair Ellinor"*

Now crimson'd is the cheek of dawn,
Bright pearls her tresses twine,
And I am here at break of morn
To be your valentine.

Then up he rose and donn'd his clothes,
And dupp'd the chamber door;
Let in the maid, that out a maid
Never departed more.

By Gis and by Saint Charity,
Alack, and fie for shame!
Young men will do't, if they come to't;
By cock, they are to blame.

Quoth she, before you tumbled me,
You promis'd me to wed.
So would I ha' done, by yonder sun,
Hadst thou not come to my bed.

GREEN GROW'TH THE HOLLY

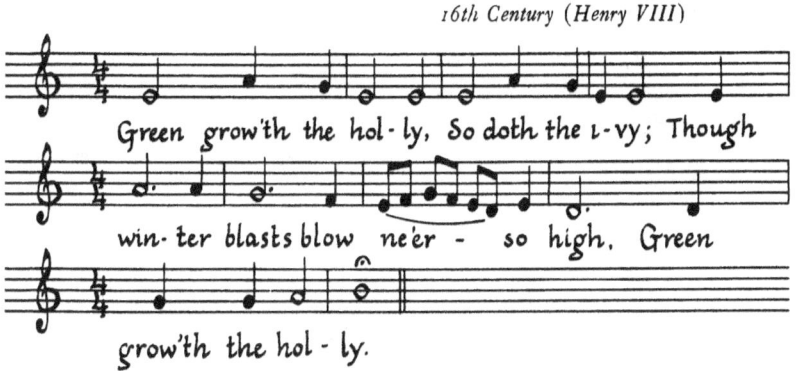

16th Century (Henry VIII)

Green grow'th the hol-ly, So doth the i-vy; Though win-ter blasts blow ne'er - so high, Green grow'th the hol-ly.

    Gay are the flowers,
    Hedgerows and ploughlands;
    The days grow longer in the sun,
    Soft fall the showers.

    Full gold the harvest,
    Grain for thy labor;
    With God must work for daily bread,
    Else, man, thou starvest.

    Fast fall the shed leaves,
    Russet and yellow;
    But resting buds are snug and safe
    Where swung the dead leaves.

    Green grow'th the holly,
    So doth the ivy;
    The God of life can never die,
    Hope! saith the holly.

THE HAWTHORNE AND THE MAID

Words from Ritson's *Ancient Songs* Air—*"The Caledonian Hunt's Delight"*

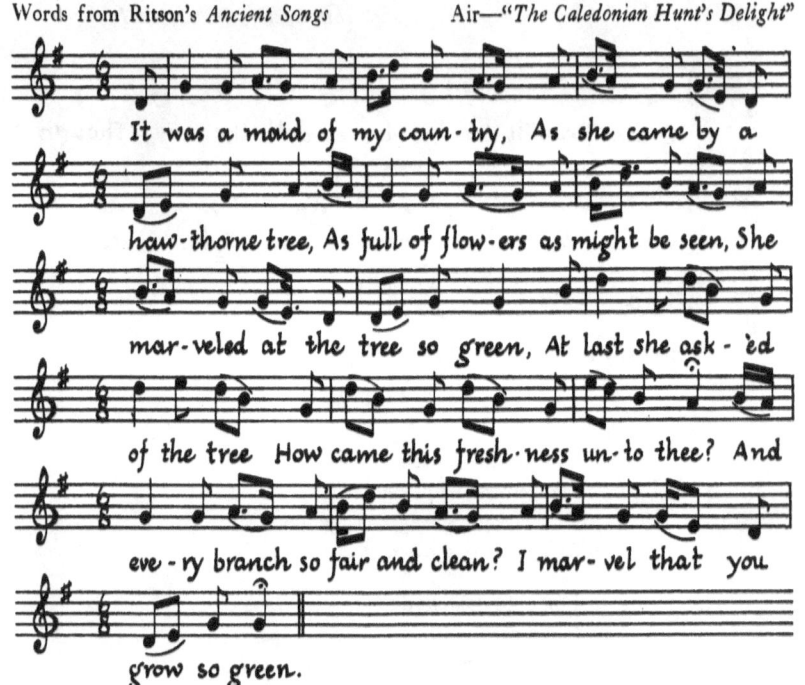

It was a maid of my country, As she came by a haw-thorne tree, As full of flow-ers as might be seen, She mar-veled at the tree so green, At last she ask-ed of the tree How came this fresh-ness un-to thee? And eve-ry branch so fair and clean? I mar-vel that you grow so green.

The tree made answer by and by,
I've cause to grow triumphantly,
The sweetest dew that e'er was seen
Doth fall on me to keep me green.
Yea, quoth the maid, but when you grow
You stand at hand at every blow,
Of every man for to be seen, . . .
I marvel that you grow so green.

Though many one take flowers from me,
And many a branch out of my tree,
I have such store they'll not be seen,
For more and more my twigs grow green. . . .
But if they chance to cut thee down
And take thy branches to the town?
Then they will never more be seen
To grow again so fresh and green..

Though that you do, it is no boot,
Although they cut me to the root,
Next year again I will be seen
To bud my branches fresh and green.
And you, fair maid, cannot do so;
For when your beauty once does go,
Then will it never more be seen,
As I with branches can grow green.

HEART'S-EASE

Thomas Rychardes (c. 1560) — Old Melody

Sing care away with sport and play, Pastime is all our pleasure; If well we fare, for nought we care, In mirth consists our treasure. Let lank-ies lurk and drudges work, We do defy their slav'ry. He's but a fool that goes to school, All we delight in brav'ry.

What doth avail far hence to sail,
And lead our life in toiling?
Or to what end should we here spend
Our days in irksome moiling?
It is the best to live at rest,
And take as God doth send it;
To haunt each wake and mirth to make,
And with good fellows spend it.

HOW SHOULD I YOUR TRUE LOVE KNOW

Cf. Ophelia's Song in *Hamlet*　　　Old Melody

And how should I your true love know from many an-other one? O by his cock-le hat and staff, And by his san-dal shoon.

He is dead and gone, lady,
He is dead and gone.
At his head a grass green turf,
At his heels a stone.

White his shroud as the mountain snow,
Larded with sweet flowers;
Which bewept to the grave did go
With true-love showers.

I LOATHE THAT I DID LOVE

Cf. The Gravedigger's Song in *Hamlet*　　　Traditional air

I loathe that I did love, In youth that I thought sweet, As time re-quires for my be-hove (For my be-hove) Me-thinks it is not meet, Me-thinks, me-thinks it is not meet.

My lusts they do me leave,
My fancies all are fled,
And tract of time begins to weave
　(Begins to weave)
Gray hairs upon my head—
　—Gray hairs, gray hairs upon my head.

For age with stealing steps
Hath clawed me in his clutch,
And lusty youth away he leaps
　(Away he leaps)
As there had been no such—
　—As there, as there had been no such.

　　　A pickax and a spade,
　　　And eke a shrouding sheet,
　　　A house of clay for to be made
　　　　(For to be made)
　　　For such a guest most meet—
　　　　—For such, for such a guest most meet.

IN SAD AND ASHY WEEDS

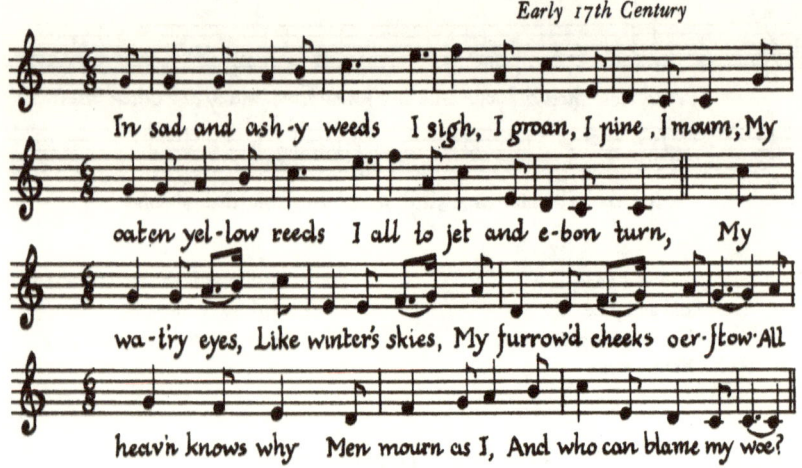

Early 17th Century

In sad and ash-y weeds I sigh, I groan, I pine, I mourn; My oaten yel-low reeds I all to jet and e-bon turn, My wa-try eyes, Like winter's skies, My furrow'd cheeks oer-flow. All heav'n knows why Men mourn as I, And who can blame my woe?

In sable robes of night,
My days of joy apparelled be,
My sorrows see no light,
My light through sorrows nothing see.
For now my sun
His date hath run
And from his sphere doth go,
To endless bed
Of folded lead,
And who can blame my woe?

My flocks I now forsake,
That silly sheep my griefs may know,
And lilies loath to take
That since his fall presum'd to grow.
I envy air
Because it dare
Still breathe and he not so;
Hate earth that doth
Entomb his youth,
And who can blame my woe?

JOHN ANDERSON, MY JO

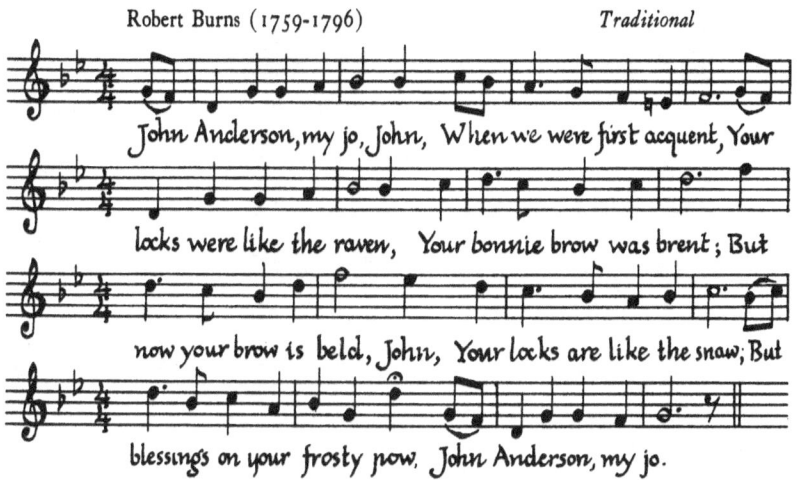

Robert Burns (1759-1796)   *Traditional*

John Anderson, my jo, John, When we were first acquent, Your locks were like the raven, Your bonnie brow was brent; But now your brow is beld, John, Your locks are like the snow; But blessings on your frosty pow, John Anderson, my jo.

John Anderson, my jo, John,
We clamb the hill thegither,
And mony a canty day, John,
We've had wi' ane anither;
Now we maun totter down, John,
But hand in hand we'll go;
And sleep thegither at the foot,
John Anderson, my jo.

THE LORD AT FIRST DID ADAM MAKE

Old Christmas Carol

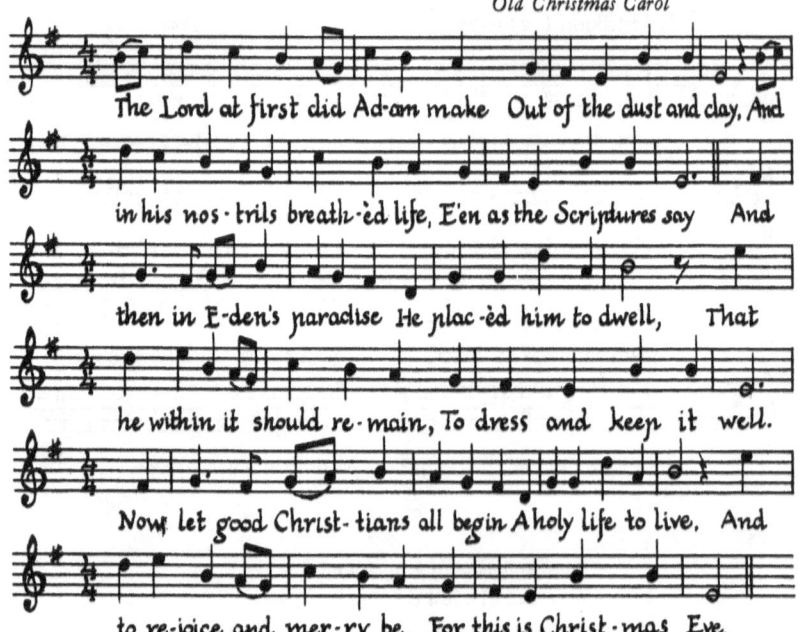

The Lord at first did Adam make Out of the dust and clay, And in his nostrils breathèd life, E'en as the Scriptures say And then in Eden's paradise He placèd him to dwell, That he within it should remain, To dress and keep it well. Now let good Christians all begin A holy life to live, And to rejoice and merry be, For this is Christmas Eve.

And thus within the garden he
  Commanded was to stay;
And unto him in commandment
  These words the Lord did say,
"The fruit that in the garden grows
  To thee shall be for meat,
Except the tree in midst thereof,
  Of which thou shalt not eat."

Now let good Christians, etc.

"For in that day thou dost it touch,
  Or dost it then come nigh,
And if that thou dost eat thereof,
  Then thou shalt surely die."
But Adam he did take no heed
  To that same holy thing,
But did transgress God's holy laws,
  And sore was wrapp'd in sin.

Now let good Christians, etc.

Now mark the goodness of the Lord,
  Which He to mankind bore;
His mercy soon He did extend
  Lost man for to restore;
And then, for to redeem our souls
  From death, and hell and thrall,
He said His own dear Son should come
  The Saviour of us all.

Now let good Christians, etc.

And now the tide is nigh at hand
  In which our Saviour came,
Let us rejoice and merry be
  In keeping of the same.
Let's feed the poor and hungry sort,
  And such as do it crave;
And when we die, in Heaven be sure
  Our reward we shall have.

Now let good Christians, etc.

LORD GREGORY

"Oh, open the door, Lord Gregory, Oh, open and let me in. The rain rains on my yellow hair, The dew-drops o'er my chin."
"If you are the lass of Lochroyan, As I trow you are not she, Now tell me some of the love tokens, That past between thee and me."

"Oh, open the door, Lord Gregory,
  Oh, open the door, I pray!
For thy young son is in my arms,
  And will be dead ere day."
When the cock had crawn, and the day did dawn,
  And the sun began to peep,
Then up and raise him Lord Gregory,
  And sair, sair did he weep.

"Oh, I ha'e dreamed a dream, mother,
  I wish it may prove true!
That the bonny lass of Lochroyan
  Was at the gate e'en now."
"If it be for the lass of Lochroyan
  That ye make a' this din—
She stood a' last night at your door,
  But I trow she won not in."

"O woe betide you, ill woman,
  An ill death may ye die!
That wouldna open the door to her
  Nor yet would waken me."
The wind blew loud, the sea grew rough,
  And dashed the boat on shore;
Fair Annie floated through the foam,
  But the baby rose no more.

O cherry, cherry was her cheek,
  And golden was her hair,
But clay-cold were her rosy lips,
  No spark of life was there.
And first he kissed her cherry cheek,
  And syne he kissed her chin,
And syne he kissed her rosy lips,
  There was no breath within.

THE MAN THAT LIVES MUST LEARN TO DIE

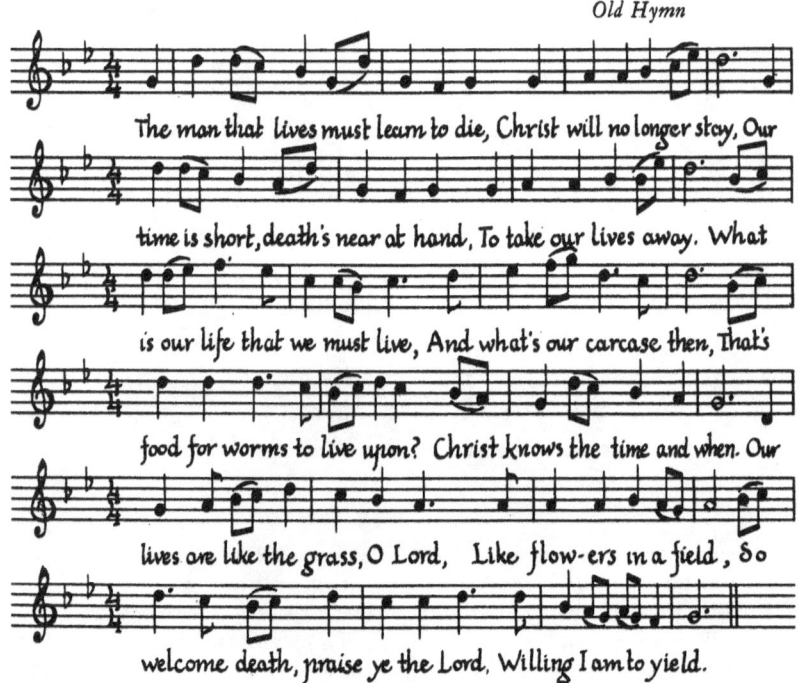

Old Hymn

The man that lives must learn to die, Christ will no longer stay, Our time is short, death's near at hand, To take our lives away. What is our life that we must live, And what's our carcase then, That's food for worms to live upon? Christ knows the time and when. Our lives are like the grass, O Lord, Like flow-ers in a field, So welcome death, praise ye the Lord, Willing I am to yield.

Now we must die and leave this world,
    That we have lived in,
Nothing but our poor winding sheet,
    To wrap our bodies in.
The bitter plagues, the fiery hell,
    Where sinners they are slain!
His beast shall die, his sheep shall rot,
    Cold clay shall be his grave.
Besides, himself sickness shall have,
    No physic shall him cure,
He ne'er shall live to see old age,
    His life will not endure.

MY LOVE WAS BORN IN ABERDEEN

I'll sell my rock, my reel, my tow,
My gude grey mare and hawkit cow,
To buy myself a tartan plaid,
To follow the boy wi' the White Cockade.

Oh, he's a ranting, roving lad, etc.

O MORTAL MAN, REMEMBER WELL

Sussex Mummer's Carol

A glorious angel from heaven came, Unto a virtuous maid, Strange tidings and great news of joy the humble Mary had. The humble Mary had.

O mortal man, remember well
When Christ our Lord was born,
He was crucified betwixt two thieves
And crownèd with the thorn.
(And crownèd with the thorn.)

O mortal man, remember well
When Christ died on the rood:
'Twas for our sins and wicked ways
Christ shed His precious blood.
(Christ shed His precious blood.)

O mortal man, remember well
When Christ was wrapped in clay,
He was taken to a sepulchre
Where no man ever lay.
(Where no man ever lay.)

God bless the mistress of this house
With gold chain round her breast;
Where e'er her body sleeps or wakes,
Lord send her soul to rest.
(Lord send her soul to rest.)

God bless the master of this house
With happiness beside;
Where e'er his body rides or walks,
Lord Jesus be his guide.
(Lord Jesus be his guide.)

God bless your house, your children too,
Your cattle and your store;
The Lord increase you day by day,
And give you more and more.
(And give you more and more.)

THE ROMISH LADY

Old Hymn Ballad

There was a Rom-ish la-dy brought up in po-pe-ry,
Her mother al-ways taught her the priest she must obey;
"O pardon me, dear mo-ther, I hum-bly pray thee now,
For un-to these false i-dols I can no longer bow."

Assisted by her handmaid, a Bible she conceal'd,
And there she gain'd instruction, till God his love reveal'd;
No more she prostrates herself to pictures deck'd with gold,
But soon she was betray'd and her Bible from her stol'd.

"I'll bow to my dear Jesus, I'll worship God unseen,
I'll live by faith for ever, the works of men are vain;
I cannot worship angels, nor pictures made by men;
Dear mother, use your pleasure, but pardon if you can."

With grief and great vexation, her mother straight did go
T' inform the Roman clergy the cause of all her woe:
The priests were soon assembled, and for the maid did call,
And forced her in the dungeon, to fright her soul withal.

The more they strove to fright her, the more she did endure,
Although her age was tender, her faith was strong and sure.
The chains of gold so costly they from this lady took,
And she with all her spirits, the pride of life forsook.

Before the pope they brought her, in hopes of her return,
And there she was condemned in horrid flames to burn.
Before the place of torment they brought her speedily,
With lifted hands to heaven she then agreed to die.

There being many ladies assembled at the place,
She raised her eyes to heaven, and begg'd supplying grace.
"Weep not, ye tender ladies, shed not a tear for me—
While my poor body's burning, my soul the Lord shall see.

"Yourselves you need to pity, and Zion's deep decay.
Dear ladies, turn to Jesus, no longer make delay."
In comes her raving mother, her daughter to behold,
And in her hands she brought her pictures deck'd with gold,

"O take from me these idols, remove them from my sight;
Restore to me my Bible, wherein I take delight.
Alas, my aged mother, why on my ruin bent?
'Twas you that did betray me, but I was innocent.

"Tormentors, use your pleasure, and do as you think best—
I hope my blessed Jesus will take my soul to rest."
Soon as these words were spoken, up steps the man of death,
And kindled up the fire to stop her mortal breath.

Instead of golden bracelets, with chains they bound her fast;
She cried, "My God give power—now must I die at last?
With Jesus and his angels for ever I shall dwell,
God pardon priest and people, and so I bid farewell."

THE SPANISH LADY

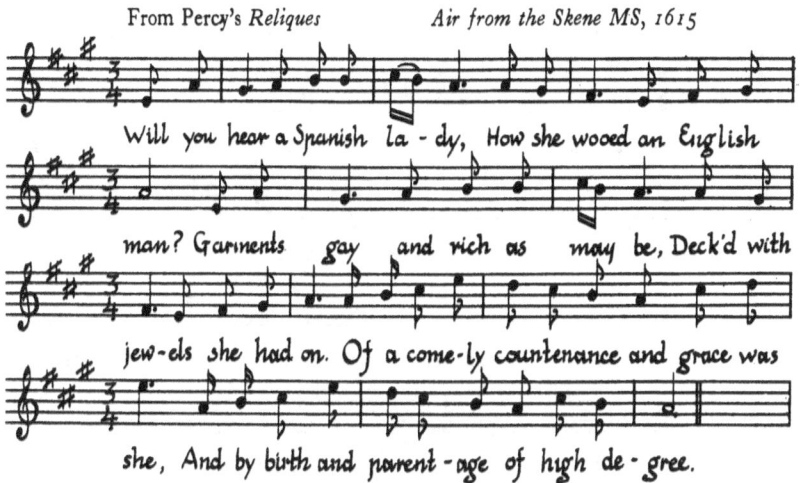

From Percy's *Reliques* Air from the Skene MS, 1615

Will you hear a Spanish la-dy, How she wooed an English man? Garments gay and rich as may be, Deck'd with jewels she had on. Of a comely countenance and grace was she, And by birth and parent-age of high de-gree.

As his pris'ner there he kept her,
In his hands her life did lie;
Cupid's bands did tie them faster
By the liking of an eye!
In his courteous company was all her joy,
To favour him in love she was not coy.

But at last there came commandment
For to set the ladies free,
With their jewels still adorned,
None to do them injury.
Then said this lady mild, "Full woe is me,
Let me still sustain this kind captivity."

TAKE, OH TAKE THOSE LIPS AWAY

Beaumont and Fletcher,
Shakespeare
John Gallard (1687-1749)

Take, oh, take those lips a-way. That so sweet-ly were forsworn; And those eyes, the break of day, Lights that do mis-lead the morn. But my kisses bring again, Seals of love, though sealed in vain; But my kis-ses bring again, Seals of love though sealed in vain.

Wrapped in barren drifts of snow,
   Scarce a favor winter wears,
Cold his heart, like thine, doth grow,
   Chill the welcome that he bears.
Melt, oh melt and set me free,
Bound in icy chains by thee;
Melt, oh melt and set me free,
Bound in icy chains by thee.

Hide, oh hide those hills of snow,
   Which thy frozen bosom bears,
On whose tops the pinks that grow
   Are of those that April wears—
But first set my poor heart free,
Bound in those icy chains by thee;
But first set my poor heart free,
Bound in those icy chains by thee.

THERE WAS A LADY LOVED A SWINE

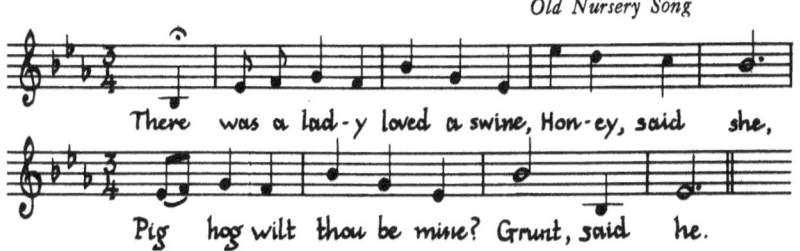

I'll build thee a silver sty,
    Honey, said she,
And in it thou shalt lie—
    Grunt, said he.

And pinned with a silver pin,
    Honey, said she,
That thou mayst go out and in—
    Grunt, said he.

Wilt thou then have me now,
    Honey? said she.
Speak or my heart will break—
    Grunt, said he.

THE THREE RAVENS

Old Ballad

Down, down in yonder green field,
    Down and down, hey down, hey down,
There lies a knight slain on his shield.
    With a down ———.
His hounds they lie down at his feet,
So well they their master keep.
    With a down, derry, derry, derry, down, down.

His hawks they fly so eagerly,
    Down and down, hey down, hey down,
There's no fowl dare come him nigh.
    With a down ———.
Down, down, there came a fallow doe,
As great with young as she might go.
    With a down, derry, derry, derry, down, down.

She liftit up his bloody head,
   Down and down, hey down, hey down,
And kissed his wounds that were so red.
   With a down ——.
She got him up upon her back,
And carried him to earthen lake.
   With a down, derry, derry, derry, down, down.

She buried him before the prime,
   Down and down, hey down, hey down,
She was dead herself ere even-song time.
   With a down ——.
God send to every gentlemen,
Such hawks, such hounds and such a leman.
   With a down, derry, derry, derry, down, down.

TOMORROW SHALL BE MY DANCING DAY

Old Folk Carol

To-mor-row shall be my dan-cing day, I would my true love did so chance, To see the legend of my play, To call my true love to my dance. Sing oh my love, oh my love, my love, my love, This have I done for my true love.

Then was I born of a virgin pure,
Of her I took fleshly substance;
Thus was I knit to man's nature,
To call my true love to my dance.
   Sing oh my love, etc.

In a manger laid and wrapp'd I was,
So very poor, this was my chance,
Betwixt an ox and a silly poor ass,
To call my true love to my dance.
   Sing oh my love, etc.

Then afterwards baptized I was,
The Holy Ghost on me did glance,
My Father's voice heard from above,
To call my true love to my dance.
   Sing oh my love, etc.

Into the desert I was led,
Where I fasted without substance;
The devil bade me make stones my bread,
To have me break my true love's dance.
   Sing oh my love, etc.

The Jews on me they made great suit,
And with me made great variance,
Because they lov'd darkness rather than light,
To call my true love to my dance.
   Sing oh my love, etc.

For thirty pence Judas me sold,
His covetousness for to advance;
Mark whom I kiss, the same do hold,
The same is he shall lead the dance.
   Sing oh my love, etc.

Before Pilate the Jews me brought,
Where Barabbas had deliverance,
They scourg'd me and set me at nought,
Judged me to die to lead the dance.
   Sing oh my love, etc.

Then on the cross hanged I was,
Where a spear to my heart did glance,
There issued forth both water and blood,
To call my true love to my dance.
   Sing oh my love, etc.

Then down to hell I took my way
For my true love's deliverance,
And rose again on the third day,
Up to my true love to the dance.
   Sing oh my love, etc.

Then up to heaven I did ascend
Where now I dwell in sure substance,
On the right hand of God, that man
May come unto the general dance.
   Sing oh my love, etc.

'TWAS ON THAT DARK, THAT DOLEFUL NIGHT

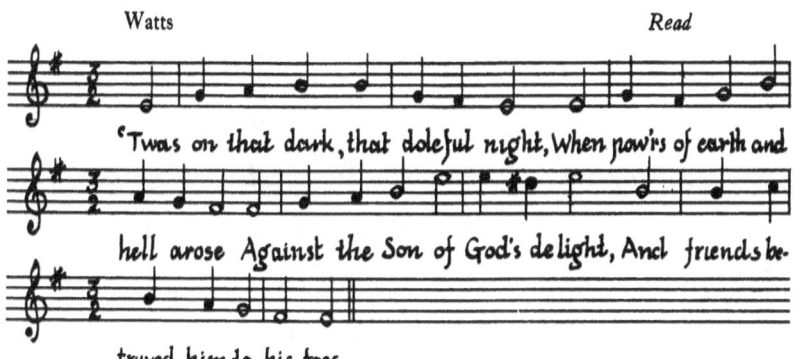

Watts — Read

'Twas on that dark, that doleful night, When pow'rs of earth and hell arose Against the Son of God's delight, And friends betrayed him to his foes.

Before the mournful scene began,
He took the bread, and blest, and brake,
What love through all his actions ran!
What wondrous words of grace he spake!

"This is my body, broke for sin;
Receive and eat the living food";
Then took the cup and blessed the wine;
"'Tis the new covenant in my blood."

"Do this," he cried, "till time shall end,
In memory of your dying friend;
Meet at my table, and record
The love of your exalted Lord."

THE TWELVE BLESSINGS OF MARY

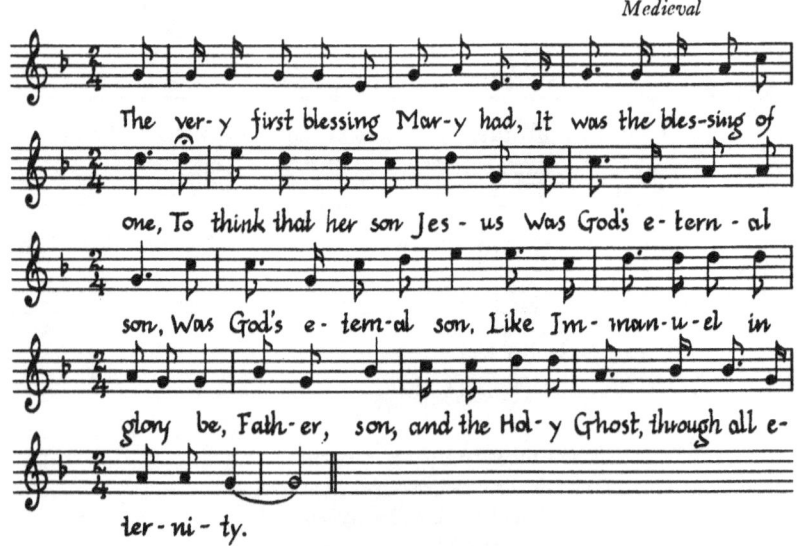

Medieval

The ver-y first blessing Mar-y had, It was the bles-sing of one, To think that her son Jes-us Was God's e-tern-al son, Was God's e-tern-al son, Like Im-man-u-el in glory be, Fath-er, son, and the Hol-y Ghost, through all e-ter-ni-ty.

(For each verse sing as the first verse, substituting the following lines for lines two, four, and five.)

2.... It was the blessing of two... Could read the Bible through....

3.... It was the blessing of three... Could set the prisoners free....

4.... It was the blessing of four... Could turn the rich to poor

5.... It was the blessing of five... Could raise the dead alive....

6.... It was the blessing of six... Could bear the crucifix....

7.... It was the blessing of seven... Could carry the keys of heaven....

8.... It was the blessing of eight... Could make the crooked straight....

9.... It was the blessing of nine... Could turn the water to wine....

10.... It was the blessing of ten... Could write without a pen....

11.... It was the blessing of eleven... Could open the gates of heaven....

12.... It was the blessing of twelve... Could open the gates of hell....

WESTRON WIND

Mart'mas wind when wilt thou blow?
  (The small rain down can rain.)
The green leaves fall from off the trees,
  And I to my love do call in vain.

Westron wind when wilt thou blow?
  (The small rain down can rain.)
Christ, that my love were in my arms,
  And I in my bed again!

WHEN MAGGIE AND I WAS ACQUAINT

To Maggie my love did I tell—
    Saut tears did my passion express.
Alas, for I lo'ed her o'er well,
    And the women lo'e sic a man less.
Her heart it was frozen and cauld,
    Her pride had my ruin decreed;
Therefore I will wander abroad,
    And lay my banes far fra the Tweed.

GLOSSARY

aboon—above
aft—often
ban (feminine, *bhan*)—fair
bairn (bairnie)—baby
bannocks — bread, larger than cakes
bearmeal—barley-meal
beld—bald
bleese—blaze
bonnie—beautiful
bothy—a shepherd's hut
braw—beautiful, brave
brent—high, smooth
brulzie—broil, fight
burd—maiden
burnie—streamlet
canty—cheerful, lively
cockle—bearing the cockle-shell of a pilgrim
claymore—two-edged broadsword
coof—fool, ninnie
corrie—a circular hollow in a hillside
dool—sorrow
dorty—saucy
dup—open
ee (e'e)—eye
een—eyes
fallow—pale brownish color
faulding—folding (of sheep)
gang—go

gear—wealth, goods
gowd (goud)—gold
greet—weep
hawkit—white-faced (cow)
jo—sweetheart, joy
jow—to swing and ring
knowe—knoll, hillock
kye—cows
lard—strew, bedeck
leman—mistress
loun—rascal
maun—must
mavis—thrush
meickle—much
mergens—myriad, many
minnie—mother
overcome—the refrain of a song
pow—head, poll
rock—distaff
routh (rowth)—abundance
rowe—roll
scrubblin—a ne'er-do-well, a lazy fellow
shoon—shoes
soy—silk
syne—then, thereafter
thegither—together
toom—empty
trow—believe
waefu'—woeful
wae worth—woe befall
yowe—ewe

FAYETTEVILLE HISTORICAL CELEBRATION

John A. Oates, *General Chairman*
Charles G. Rose, *President*

1739 * 1939

IN COLLABORATION WITH

The CAROLINA PLAYMAKERS
Frederick H. Koch, *Director*

PRESENTS

The Highland Call

A Symphonic Drama of American History

— BY —

PAUL GREEN

DIRECTED BY

JOHN W. PARKER

Settings by Elmer Hall *Costumes by* Ora Mae Davis

FIRST PRODUCTION

LaFayette Opera House, Fayetteville, N. C.
NOVEMBER 20, 21, 22, 23, 24, 1939

Memorial Hall, Chapel Hill, N. C.
DECEMBER 5 AND 6, 1939

THE CHARACTERS
(In Order of Their Appearance)

Mr. Mac	Earl Wynn
A British Officer	Charles Avery
A Man	George Wilson
A Boy	Charles Williams
First Soldier	Willis Gould
Second Soldier	Don Pope
A Clerk	George Grotz
Allan MacDonald	Maurice Edwards
Flora MacDonald	Margaret Holmes
Sandy Ochiltree	Donald Mason
Peggy MacNeill	Elizabeth Carr
The Mayor	Weider Sievers
Dan Murchison	Douglass Watson
Rev. John MacLeod	Charles Parrish
A Captain	John Roeder
Anne MacLeod	Elizabeth Blair
Alexander MacLeod	Howard Richardson
A Messenger	Jimmie DeVane
Alexander MacDonald	David Hooks
James MacDonald	Russell Rogers
Donald MacDonald	Robert Carroll
Jennie Bhan MacNeill	Josephine Sharkey
Colonel Alexander MacAllister	Weider Sievers
Old Joe, *An Indian*	C. Wallace Jackson
A Workman	Lawrence Patten
A Watchman	George Grotz
Farquhar Campbell	Joe Morrison
Old Hugh MacDonald	George Wilson
Dave Fanning	Theodore Dichter
A Messenger	Sanford Reece

Townspeople: Betty Pope, Catherine Mallory, Evelyn Matthews, Mary Wood, Mary Elizabeth Rhyne, Connie Smith, Hilda Sharkey, Irene Wynn, Ralph Lutrin, Garland Peterson, Bill Brasmer, Terry Holmes, William Hedgpeth, Jr., Herman Vander Molen, John Monoghan, Jacob Ward, Quincy Nimocks, III, Claude Rankin, Jr.

Highland Dancers: Evon Eldridge, Ellen Coxe Merritt, Neill McNair, Gene MacLeod, Dorothy Brooks, Ruth Stuart, Rebecca Rogers, Jean MacNeill Boyer.

THE SCENES

Time: 1752-1776   Place: Scotland and America

ACT I

Scene 1. A corridor in a military post, Scotland. 1752.
Scene 2. The wharf at Campbelltown, Scotland. An August afternoon, 1774.
Scene 3. The woods near Killiegray, Flora MacDonald's home in North Carolina. Several months later.

Intermission.

ACT II

Scene 1. A garden near the State House in Gross Creek (now Fayetteville). Several days later.
Scene 2. The arcade of the State House. The following day.
Scene 3. The living room at Killiegrey. Several months later.

THE MUSIC

¶ *Music in the play selected by the Author from old Scotch folk songs, ballads, dances, and hymns.*
¶ *Choral arrangements by J. Wilgus Eberly.*
¶ *Organ arrangements by Jan Philip Schinhan.*
¶ *Choir under the direction of Virginia Harlin.*
¶ *Dances directed by Ethel Bateman.*
¶ *At the organ, Jan Philip Schinhan.*

THE HIGHLAND CALL CHORUS

Sopranos:
  Kate DeCamp
  Louise Herndon
  Billie Burgess
  Anne McInnis
  Pearl McFadyen
  Jessie Lehman
  Harriet Vickery
  Edith McLean

Tenors:
  Orva Perkins
  Herman Stephens
  Charlie Scott
  Jimmy Guthrie
  A. M. Lehman

Altos:
  Sarah Harry
  Elise Hood
  Kate McGeachy
  Cecelia MacKethan
  Dottie Brown
  Rebecca Byrd
  Annie McGugan
  Melrose Blette

Basses:
  W. A. VanStory
  M. G. Joslin
  Ed Plummer
  Hector McGeachy
  Vivian Hollinshed
  Parker Vickery

¶ *The scenery executed by students of the Dramatic Art Department of the University of North Carolina, under the supervision of Elmer Hall.*
¶ *The costumes designed by Ora Mae Davis and executed under her supervision with the assistance of Lynette Heldman, Irene Smart, Betty Pope, Mary Coley, Mary Louise Boylston, Barry Lynn, and Virginia Reece.*
¶ *The properties designed by Walter Preston and executed with the assistance of students of the Dramatic Art Technical courses.*

Assistant to the Director
        Terrell O. Everett
General Stage Manager
        Frederick Walsh

Stage Manager
                Larry Wismer
Lighting, Paul Quinn
Properties, Joe Bouldin
Make-Up, Lynette Heldman

THE PLAYMAKERS STAFF

Frederick H. Koch	*Director*
Paul Green	*Playwright and Literary Advisor*
Samuel Selden	*Associate Director*
Elmer Hall	*Technical Director*
John W. Parker	*Assistant Director and Business Manager*
Earl Wynn	*Assistant Director*
Ora Mae Davis	*Director of Costuming*
Lynette Heldman	*Assistant Director of Costuming*
Frederick Walsh	*General Stage Manager*
Larry Wismer	*Assistant Technical Director*
Frank Guess	*Assistant to the Director*
Catherine Mallory	*Assistant in Experimental Production*
Wootten-Moulton	*Photographers*

FAYETTEVILLE HISTORICAL CELEBRATION, INC.

CHARLES G. ROSE, President
THOMAS M. HUNTER, Vice-President
S. W. TOMLINSON, Secretary & Treasurer
JOHN A. OATES, Managing Director
L. R. ASHE, Executive Assistant

DIRECTORS

Judge I. M. Meekins, Elizabeth City
Harry McMullan, Raleigh
Dr. Frank P. Graham, Chapel Hill
J Bayard Clark, Fayetteville
R. O. Everett, Durham

John A. Oates, Fayetteville
Charles G. Rose, Fayetteville
Judge Henry A. Grady, New Bern
Dickson McLean, Lumberton
John H. Anderson, Raleigh

COMMITTEES

State Senate:
 T. W. M. Long, Halifax, Chairman; W. A. Graham, Lincoln; R. A. McIntyre, Robeson; K. Clyde Council, Columbus; S. B. Frink, Brunswick; Ralph Gardner, Cleveland; Fred I. Sutton, Lenoir.

House of Representatives:
 John W. Caffey, Guilford, Chairman; U. S. Page, Bladen; E. B. McNeill, Hoke; Frank McNeill, Robeson; D. Lacy McBryde, Cumberland; B. B. Everett, Halifax.

University of North Carolina:
 Josephus Daniels, Judge John J. Parker, Judge Francis D. Winston, O. Max Gardner, Henry M. London, Clyde A. Erwin.

COMMITTEE CHAIRMEN FOR FAYETTEVILLE HISTORICAL CELEBRATION, Inc.

Publicity, George Myrover
Constitution Ratification
  Col. Terry A. Lyon
University of North Carolina
  C. W. Rankin, Sr.
Masonic, Q. J. Scarborough
Military, Major J. A. Helms
Parade & Decorations
  P. C. Duckworth
Finance, T. M. Hunter
Municipal, Donald McQueen
Reception and Entertainment
  Oscar P. Breece
Hotels, Gilbert A. Martin
Police & Parking
  A. B. Crews
Marshals
  Thomas W. Rankin

Athletics, Thomas A. DeVane
Museum, Mrs. W. T. Brock
Scottish Register
  Mrs. Margaret O'Rourke
Opera House, F. D. Byrd
Music, Joe Hamrick
Schools, Horace Sisk
Scottish Clans
  W. S. McRae
  Joseph S. Huske
Beautification
  Mrs. C. C. McAllister
Street Sales
  John W. Hensdale
Scotch Marker, W. M. Shaw
Scotch Amusements
  Thomas H. Sutton, III
  Capt. T. J. Sands, 83rd F. A.

www.ingramcontent.com/pod-product-compliance
Lightning Source LLC
Chambersburg PA
CBHW021354290426
44108CB00010B/243